SET FREE

SHARON CRICK

Copyright © 2024 by Sharon Crick

All rights reserved. No part of this book may be reproduced or transmitted in any form or by any means, electronic or mechanical, including photocopying, recording, or by any information storage and retrieval system, without permission in writing from the copyright owner.

Australian Self Publishing Group, Pty. Ltd / Inspiring Publishers
PO Box 159, Calwell, ACT 2905
Australia. Phone: 61-(0) 2 6291-2904
http://australianselfpublishinggroup.com

Member of the:
Australian Publishers Association.
International Book Publishing Association.
The Small Press Network

Author: Sharon Crick

Young/Old adult
Non-Fiction
Crick / SET FREE/ 1

Title: **SET FREE**

ISBN: 978-1-923087-32-3 (print)

Contents

Preface 5
Acknowledgement 7
Introduction 9
Afterword 11
Author's Biography 13
Chapter 1: The Train Station 15
Chapter 2: Reformatory 28
Chapter 3: Holidays (1973) 39
Chapter 4: Home For Good (1974) 46
Chapter 5: More Drama 53
Chapter 6: Sharon 57
Chapter 7: Arrested 67
Chapter 8: Getting Married 75
Chapter 9: Tent Campaign (1981) 79
Chapter 10: Testimonies/Challenges 85
        Part Two: Testimonies/Challenges 95
Chapter 11: GOD Blessed Me 103
Chapter 12: Many Places/Countries 111
        Part Two: Many Places/Countries 122
Chapter 13: The Grace of GOD 129
Chapter 14: The Overcomer 134
Reference 137
Epilogue 138

A True Story

*"To GOD be the glory
for the things He hath done."*

Preface

Meeting the character of the book at the age of seventeen, I had no idea that two years later he would became my husband. Our first meeting was unplanned; we were both on our own schedules. When we set eyes on each other for the first time, it was love at first sight. The unexplainable happened, and we stared at each other for a few seconds. The stare seemed to ask, "Where have you been all this time?" Months later, we met again. This time, the character asked to be introduced to me. We began dating, and most of our time together was spent listening to his stories about his violent gang life, survival against enemies, hard years in a reformatory, hardships, challenges, and shortcomings. He lived his life on the edge.

I loved him deeply, and my empathy for him grew stronger. His stories were captivating, making me laugh, cry, feel sad, happy, anxious, and angry. Sometimes, in the middle of a story, I was so moved that I would find myself hugging him, saying, "I am so sorry." Later in life, I decided to take on the challenge of sharing his story with the world. I studied in New Zealand, received a bachelor's degree in early childhood education, and further studied for two more years to receive my teacher's registration. I took on various roles in many early childhood centres, implementing my practice. I served as a supervisor, lead educator, team leader, organised educational events for young children, and was an associate teacher for students in training. Noticing my strength in these roles, I enjoyed documenting children's learning. In 2012, our family relocated to Australia. It was here that I was inspired to write young children's books, documenting their learning from their perspective.

SET FREE

Married for forty-four years, I have witnessed the transformative power of GOD in my husband's life. We have faced many struggles and challenges together, but GOD had a plan for our lives. I, too, am born again and have seen GOD's love and power in my own life, in my children, and in their children. From a teaching perspective, a child's learning and development are fundamental. As parents, creating the right environment will allow a child to thrive confidently. Unfortunately, for some of us, it was beyond our reach. We did not grow up in a safe, nurturing environment; nothing was created for us to feel safe. We felt safe in our homes, with our families, but out there, we were surrounded by violence, gang wars, domestic violence, alcohol, drugs, peer pressure, gambling, and unemployment, leaving us with few choices or options.

Reformatory was a correctional institution for the treatment, training, and social rehabilitation of young, coloured offenders, expected to reform. In the character's life, GOD came and transformed him. Only Jesus Christ can make the difference. Accepting Him into your life and making Him a priority will ensure that the plans He has for us will come to pass, no matter how big the storm or trial you face.

Set Free will encourage your walk with Christ no matter what you are going through right now. I remember in December 2022, my husband did a video sharing a positive New Year message with our family: "GOD will take care of us from the beginning of the year till the end of the year." The Bible says in Deuteronomy 11:12: "A land which the LORD thy GOD careth for: the eyes of the LORD are always upon it, from the beginning of the year even unto the end of the year." In 2022, our family faced small and big waves, high and low mountains, down the valley, and up the mountain. We felt surrounded by a severe storm until the end of the year. I can say GOD did take care of us from the beginning of the year till the end. GOD was with us during the storm.

We are trusting GOD for complete healing. This year, 2024, I believe this is the season GOD placed it in my heart to share my husband's story. To the reader, be blessed when you read **Set Free**. Know in your heart that Christ can and will do the impossible in your life, granting you a breakthrough, whatever you are trusting Him for, and setting you free.

Acknowledgement

Firstly, I would like to thank the Lord Jesus Christ with all my heart and soul for making this project possible, for leading, guiding, and giving me direction and GODly wisdom.

Thank you to my husband, Brian. I love you very much and cherish our lives together. Thank you, Brian, for all your time, effort, and support in helping me get this project together. I appreciate you, and thank you for sharing all your spiritual, inspirational thoughts referring to the word of GOD. I have benefited spiritually so much from you; you have been a spiritual blessing to me and our children. Thank you for always being there for me and the children, sharing the word of GOD, encouraging us, and letting us know that the will of GOD is His word, and providing GODly counsel when needed.

Thank you to Wency, Publishing Coordinator, ASPG & Inspiring Publishers. Thank you for your support, guidance, patience, and for not making anything I envisioned for my novel seem impossible.

To my children, thank you Liesel and Amiro, Lydia, Seth and Jess, Sarah and David, for always being a helping hand in my teaching profession and getting involved. Sarah, my daughter, thank you for the beautiful photography. This novel comes as a surprise to you all, and I know you are going to enjoy reading it. To my grandchildren, Jared and Rachel, Carli, Jaden, Carter, Levi, Malachi, and Jordy, I am so thankful to GOD for all of you. This is a novel you are going to treasure always, and as you grow older, it will become more meaningful to you.

SET FREE

Thank you to my dearest mother, Maureen, for always saying the most encouraging words to me and being so supportive in whatever I do. I love you, Mum.

To the assistant manager Lodie of Australian Self-publishing Group, a special thank you for being interested in my book description. Assuring me it fitted in with The genre's you publish and encouraging me getting it out into the world.

GOD bless you all,
Sharon Crick

Introduction

B rian grew up as a child in the apartheid era, a time when white supremacy was in full control in South Africa. During his adolescence, his environment was marred by alcohol and drug-related violence, crime, and gang activity. These surroundings had a significant impact on Brian, leading to struggles at school and frequent truancy. Negative peer influence became pervasive, resulting in poor choices and behaviours. Despite his desire to achieve and make the right choices, the negative influence often prevailed.

Brian chose to attend the School of Industries in Cape Town, believing it would offer him education and a trade, unaware of what lay ahead. The School of Industries was an institution for coloured boys at risk of becoming delinquent, essentially functioning as a correctional institution.

In 1971, at the age of fifteen, Brian spent three years in this reformatory. During this time, he only came home twice for holidays. The reality of the institution did not match his expectations; corporal punishment was a routine form of discipline. Mentally, Brian prepared himself for the daily challenges, immersing himself in his schooling, vocational training, and an intense exercise program. He became physically strong, confident, and learned self-defence. However, he sometimes got involved in gang violence within the reformatory, projecting an arrogant and defiant attitude for survival.

Throughout his stay, regardless of the season, Brian experienced cold showers and had only one pair of shoes per year. One year, he lost his shoes and had to go barefoot, developing calluses on his feet. In

SET FREE

winter, he suffered severe frostbite on his fingers from doing outdoor chores.

The boys were required to do hard manual labour, such as chopping tall trees into logs with hand saws. Failure to follow instructions resulted in being whipped with a cane. Upon leaving the reformatory, Brian felt bigger and better, ready to take on the world. However, returning home three years later, he found his environment had worsened.

Brian learned a welding trade, got a job, earned good money, owned a car, and enjoyed a vibrant social life. Despite this, gang violence still loomed over his life. Weapons, enemies, speed, and alcohol consumed him. In one incident, after being stabbed and bleeding profusely, Brian jumped over a bar counter, throwing bottles of alcohol to protect himself from his enemies. He was once chased by an enemy and, after being hit across the eye with an asbestos pipe, he turned to his friend and said, "If we can just catch one, just one and kill him." This was a tactic to create fear and intimidate his enemies.

One night, while lying still in the tall grass of an open field, dagger in hand, running away from a gang fight, he waited patiently for the silence after hearing police sirens and commotion nearby. Brian was in three prisons over three days and experienced trauma when he was forced to search a dead body under the command of an Afrikaans policeman. Exhausted physically and mentally, he realised he needed to settle down.

In 1978, Brian met his queen. He fell in love with her and wanted her to be his wife, the mother of his children, and to spend the rest of his life with her. They married in 1980. One day, Brian's life took a 360-degree turn when a Christian tent campaign was held in his district. He felt led to see what it was all about. Standing outside the tent, a strong spirit of conviction came over him, and he knew he had to put his life right with Christ to be **set free**.

Sharon Crick

Afterword

Before attempting to write children's books and becoming a young children's author, I always desired to write a non-fiction novel. My husband's story was always on my heart. I envisioned the novel *Set Free* on a bookstore shelf. In 2023, my husband and I visited our home country, South Africa, for six weeks. Upon returning from this trip and giving it much thought, I planned a longer break at the end of the year and into the new year. I knew within myself that 2024 was the season *Set Free* would be published. Easier said than done, it was not an easy task. It took a great deal of time to bring *Set Free* to its published stage. Time management is fundamental when aiming to complete a task and reach a goal. Writing from a spiritual perspective, I learned the three keys to have in mind: a sound mind, wisdom, and good health. Before I continue, I can never thank GOD enough for revealing these keys to me to achieve my goal.

Throughout my walk with GOD, He has always woken me up early in the morning to spend time with Him, trusting Him to meet my needs and give me what I needed spiritually. Being an early riser allowed me to write and start my day's work. A sound mind, one of the keys to one's health and wellbeing, can influence how we make our choices, giving us the ability to put strategies into place to help us achieve. A sound mind equips us with tools to bounce back from setbacks and overcome obstacles we face. Organising, planning, dividing, juggling work, family, unexpected trials, and storms can impose a delay on the satisfaction of present ideas. Time is the biggest factor a writer is challenged with. I made a written agreement with my husband, saying he would give me his time so we could document his stories together. We found ourselves

SET FREE

spending more time than usual with each other. The two of us did a road trip to Agnes Waters for a few days, enjoying some uninterrupted time without distractions. Here, we gathered the rest of my husband's stories and tied up any loose ends relating to *Set Free*. Together, we felt like a team completing a huge task. My husband was very supportive; we both knew the reason for this trip.

Going down memory lane was good for the two of us. It made us reflect on how much we had been through and appreciate the Lord Jesus Christ even more, realising He was there all the time, in every stage of our marriage and the trials we faced together. Forgiveness brought healing to those we hurt on this journey and to those who hurt us. Ephesians 4:31-32 says, "Let all bitterness, and wrath, and anger, and clamour, and evil speaking, be put away from you, with all malice: and be ye kind one to another, tender-hearted, forgiving one another, even as GOD for Christ's sake hath forgiven you." Forgiveness helped us grow spiritually and emotionally, creating a path to live our lives together with positivity and inner peace. Only GOD can place forgiveness in our hearts. Walking this Christian journey, forgiveness is one of the signs GOD has restored us, making us new through Christ Jesus. This time away strengthened our faith, marriage, and love for each other. Thank you, honey, for sharing your story, giving hope to others, and finally bringing *Set Free* to fruition.

Sharon Crick

Author's Biography

Sharon Crick is a qualified, registered early childhood teacher living in Australia. Born in South Africa, Sharon studied and graduated in this field there. She loved reading books during her school years and always aspired to be an author.

Sharon immigrated with her husband and children to New Zealand, where she continued her studies and received her diploma. She furthered her education by earning a Bachelor's degree in Early Childhood Education. Sharon later relocated to Australia with her children to join her husband, a Special Class Welder, due to work. Living in New South Wales, Sharon was inspired to document and write, observing the learning environment from a young child's perspective. Between 2012 and 2017, she published four books: Sounds, Nani Sha, Maggie, and I See. Currently, Sharon is the director of her own family day care, continuing to teach and support young children in their learning and development.

Sharon is a devoted Christian, serving GOD wholeheartedly alongside her husband. Sharon met and fell in love with her husband in 1978. They will celebrate 44 years of marriage in 2024. She is a mother to four beautiful adult children and a grandmother to seven grandchildren. Sharon's husband has had an interesting life, always sharing amazing and gripping stories that captured her attention and left a special place in her heart. Inspired by these stories, Sharon decided to share them with the world, writing her first novel, **Set Free**.

Chapter 1
The Train Station

Anxiously, I stood at the train station, looking around. Soon, my escorts would arrive. My parents sat on a nearby bench, waiting with me. Mum was a qualified nurse, working as a matron in a hospital. Dad was a builder, a qualified tradesman. At fifteen years old, I was about to board a train for a three-day journey with complete strangers. It seemed unbelievable. I was leaving Durban to travel to Cape Town, to a reformatory called Ottery School of Industries. Situated in Cape Town, Ottery was a social institution established in 1948 on a military camp for coloured boys deemed to be in danger of becoming delinquent.

The big City Hall clock ticked away, staring back at me. Mum said, "Don't worry, Brian, I will write to you." Writing would be our only form of communication. Dad looked at me and said, "Take care of yourself, son." I heard footsteps approaching in the distance. Turning around, I saw two men walking toward us. They introduced themselves to my parents, letting them know they would be my escorts. My mother and father stood up, hugged, and kissed me goodbye. My mother took my hand and gently handed me over to the escorts. They stood on either side of me, indicating we needed to make our way to the train.

As we walked closer to the train, I looked back for a final wave. My parents stood watching me and waved. Feeling anxious, I nervously stepped onto the train, not knowing what lay ahead. The two men escorted me to our coach. Inside, there were six bunk beds, stacked on top of each other, and a table. This would be our home for the next

SET FREE

three days. As the train started to move, I went over to the window and waved to my parents. I sat down and gazed out the window as the buildings sped by.

Sitting in the train brought back my early childhood memories, My mother was from Vryburg, Northern Cape. During the June school holidays, she would take me and my siblings to visit my ouma, cousins, uncles and aunts. It was an exciting, adventurous trip growing up as a young child. I was familiar with this ride.

The sleeping arrangement was that I would sleep on the middle bunk bed, while the escorts slept on the bottom bunk bed. The rules were that if I needed the toilet at night, I would be escorted. When it was time to sleep, I would be handcuffed. I spoke up for myself, saying there was no need for handcuffs. If I wanted to, I would have run away long ago. It was expected that I be handcuffed due to previous boys attempting to run away. However, the decision to go to the reformatory was my choice, and I would not attempt to run away.

Eating, washing up, and visiting the bathrooms were all I did for three long days. Gazing out the window was the highlight of the trip. I absorbed the beautiful scenery, mountains, sunset, sunrise, cattle grazing, and the places and cities we passed by. Often, my family and home would come to my thoughts. I would think of where I was going and what was it going be like. This journey gave me time to reflect on my years growing up.

We lived in a neighbourhood, in a lane with a row of houses. It was a village where families cared for each other, knew each other, and good relationships had developed among us. As young children, we would play together at each other's houses or play games in the lane. My mother was well known in the community; she always offered a helping hand to those in need, especially with her nursing skills. Whenever there was a wound or medical problem in the neighbourhood, Mum was always available to help.

My mother was a woman with principles; she was strict. The neighbourhood families had respect and admiration for her because of her care and contributions to the community. Awoken by the sound

Chapter 1

of spoons clinking and sizzling in the early hours of the morning, the smell of food would go straight to my nostrils. It was my dad, preparing his lunch for work, converting a stew into a curry. Dad loved his hot, spicy curries with chillies and curry powder, using the leftover dinner from the previous night. My mother preferred stews, steamed food, and marmalade jam. My dad was from Durban, and my mother worked at Wentworth Hospital, not far from home.

I remember at night, asleep in my bed, my mother would leave for work. Feeling a gentle peck on my cheek and sweets (jelly babies) placed in my hand, I knew she was going to work. I would see her again only the next day when she was fast asleep in her bed. I had four sisters and a baby brother. We lived in a neat, clean, and tidy three-bedroom home. Coming from a nursing background, keeping the house clean was a priority for my mother. Spring cleaning days were not my favourite. My mother would empty out the whole house and thoroughly clean each room with pride. Hygiene was important to her, followed by respect. We were always reminded how to address our elders.

On Sundays, my mother attended the Anglican church, and my sister's sang in the church choir. I attended Northgate Primary, a school in the neighbourhood. The school was very close to my house, and I would walk to school with my friends in the neighbourhood. The school had no playground; instead, the property was surrounded by red sand, which meant I always came home dirty with sand in my shoes.

I never attended a nursery school or kindergarten to prepare me for my first year at school. I always wondered how the children in my class knew and understood their schoolwork. I struggled with school and felt like I knew nothing. I probably would have been more eager to learn if I had a foundation in my early years. Math was my favourite subject and kept me going to school, but there was no motivation for the rest of the subjects. I preferred teachers who used illustrations, dramatisations, and different forms of clichés. School and the teachers became boring to me.

The care takers lived on the school premises and maintained the property. They played music, and I would always dance for them.

SET FREE

I would go home after school with no one to follow up on me. My mother worked, my sisters went to school, and they had after-school chores. Sometimes my mother would give us a special treat by buying a whole cake. She would place the cake on top of the fridge, covered to keep the flies away. Noticing the cake on the fridge, I would always be observant when the first slice was cut.

As soon as the first slice was cut, it gave me an opportunity to cut myself another slice when no one was around. The more my mother cut the cake, I felt I had the right to take another slice. As the cake got smaller, I would stop cutting to avoid being caught. Suspicion arose about who the culprit was, but nobody spoke. I loved cake, and I remember participating in a school play, "The Mouse and the Cake," by Eliza Cooke. In this play, they used a real cake, and it looked delicious. There was a group of us on stage, and we had to recite the poem. We couldn't wait for the play to end because the teacher told us we would get to eat the whole cake afterward.

One of the chores my mother delegated to me was washing the dishes. I would enter the kitchen, make noise with the dishes, leave the tap running, check if everything was clear, then slip out the back door to play with my friends. Outdoors was my only escape. We lived in an area with lots of bushes.

My friend and I would go into the bushes, set up a camp, and dig a deep square hole in the ground, deep enough for us all to sit in. We used branches and leaves to cover the hole. Our next mission was to make our own bow and arrow from the bamboo bushes so we could go hunting. We hunted in another large bush area. One day, while hunting, we saw chickens running around in the bush. We came across a chicken hanging from a branch, its leg tied to a rope, still alive. At nine and ten years old, we had no idea how to cook a chicken. Feeling like we were on a real hunting trip, we took the chicken to our camp, proud of our achievement. One of my friends killed the chicken, and we all participated in cleaning it and making a fire.

Thinking we had it all under control, we cooked the chicken on the fire for a while. We broke and shared the chicken amongst ourselves,

Chapter 1

but when I bit into my share, it was so tough I could have lost my teeth. We threw the rest of the chicken into the bush. All kinds of creatures in the bush must have had a feast on the leftover tough chicken.

Growing up as a young child, my hobbies included soccer, flying kites, playing marbles, spinning tops, and outdoor bush camping with my friends. I also enjoyed school sports, especially the 100-meter sprint race, which I often won. Although I loved the beach, my mother would not allow me to go. If she found out I had been to the beach, I would be in trouble. Being a nurse, my mother was protective and had heard of children drowning. Still, I didn't listen and one day made the wrong choice of going to the beach with my friends. The beach was within walking distance from where I lived. We would walk up a hill and, upon reaching the top, run down the steep, sandy, winding path to the beach. One day, while running at high speed, I couldn't take the bend and landed in a bush, cutting my foot on a broken bottle.

The broken bottle caused a very deep cut, leaving my flesh hanging. My friends saw the cut and, instead of taking me home, they picked me up, put me on their shoulders, and headed towards the beach. They put me down, covered my foot in sand, and went into the ocean for a swim. Sitting on the shore, cut and wounded, I watched them swim. They did not stay too long in the ocean and soon picked me up, carried me back on their shoulders. Getting closer home, I told them to take me to my neighbour's house. I was bleeding and knew this meant trouble. I thought the neighbour would just clean me up, put a band-aid on, and I would be fine without my mother knowing. However, when the neighbour saw the condition of my foot, she said, "Brian, the best person to attend to your cut is your mother." Everyone knew my mother was a nurse, and she was the person to treat my wound. I was worried about facing my mother. My friends carried me home.

When we arrived, I showed my mother my foot, which was full of sea sand. She took one look at it and was upset, shouting at me at the top of her voice. She took me by the hand, and I hopped along with her to the outside tap. She was really upset that I had disobeyed her. She opened the tap fully, placed my wounded foot under the running water, and rinsed the sand off. It was so painful. She then got medicine and poured it into my wound. The burn and pain were agonizing, and I felt like I could jump out of my skin. After treating and bandaging my wound, she informed me that I would have to stay indoors until my foot healed. This was a hard punishment because I enjoyed being with my friends and being outside the house.

I remember when I was seven years old, curious about the wall socket. The ironing was done on a table with a blanket on top, and above the table was the wall socket. My mother had just popped over to the neighbours. It was quiet in the house, and I saw this as an opportunity to climb onto the table with a hairpin and push it into the round socket holes. As soon as I pushed the hairpin in, I fell off the table and landed on the floor. The power in the house went out, and I found myself in darkness. In shock, I continued to sit on the floor. When my mother entered the house, she realised there was no power and called out for me.

She walked into the room and saw me sitting on the floor. I told her what I had done, and she was shocked, realising I could have been electrocuted. She was happy to see I was okay, feeling that GOD protected me from a fatal accident.

At the age of 12 years old, I became mischievous, rebellious, and naughty. I stopped listening to my mother and was always getting into trouble. My behaviour started to take a toll on her. One day, she became so upset with me that she took me by the hand and marched me to the police station, which was very close to our home. She told the policemen to hit me, but instead, they handed her a stick. She gave me a good hiding in front of the policemen, who eventually told her to stop. Corporal punishment was legal at the time. Feeling satisfied that she had dealt with me, she took me back home.

My friends and I always did adventurous things together. One evening, my best friend brought white sheets and said, "Brian, today we are going to frighten the neighbours. We're going to be spooks." In our time, mentioning a spook was something scary, and as children, we would be afraid.

Chapter 1

Dressing ourselves in the white sheets, we targeted a specific house where our friends lived. We couldn't wait to see the look on their faces when they saw two white spooks standing at the door. To see where we were heading, we didn't cover our faces and ran towards my friend's house. Arriving there, we looked at each other and giggled. We knocked loudly on the door, expecting one of our friends to answer, but their mom called out, "Brian and Gerald, is it you two again?" You should have seen the two spooks make a dash for it, running as fast as we could. She knew it was us getting up to mischief again.

During the festive season, it was Christmas time, and I was 13 years old. My best friend's family had all gone to the beach, leaving him home alone. He whistled for me to come to the fence. When I got to his house, he took me to a cupboard and showed me a bottle of alcohol his dad had purchased. He knew it was alcohol because he had seen his dad take a drink with friends.

He said, "Brian, this is wine. It's called Paarl Perlé," showing me the writing on the bottle. He opened the bottle and took a sip, then said, "Brian, try it. It's sweet and tastes like juice." I was hesitant at first, knowing only adults drink alcohol, but I decided to take a sip. It tasted nice, and I drank more and more until I started to feel sick and throw up. I ran home, washed my mouth, and jumped into bed. I heard my sister tell my siblings that I was sick. Hearing this, I thought to myself, "If only you knew I had alcohol." I fell into a deep sleep and woke up the next morning feeling much better. This was my first encounter with alcohol.

At this age, I was also smoking cigarettes and occasionally marijuana with my friends, though it did not agree with me. I developed an inferiority complex, especially when I was in a crowd of people. I felt strange and realised it had a negative effect on me. I was not coping and couldn't find the right balance between myself and fitting in with my friends. I gave up smoking marijuana but continued to smoke cigarettes. Doing these things was my way of impressing my friends, wanting to feel valued and accepted, and feeling like I was one of them.

One day, eight of my friends and I decided to go to the city, to the bay area along the esplanade. We all enjoyed music and singing, so we

SET FREE

took a guitar with us. Arriving at the esplanade, we found a good spot, played the guitar, and sang some songs. After singing, we decided to go for a swim in the bay. We all jumped into the water and found a log, more like a square pole. We pushed it into the water and jumped onto it. We were having so much fun, laughing as some of my friends twisted the log, making the rest of us fall off. The bay was quite deep. When I fell off with some friends, we started swimming towards the sandbank on the shore.

Suddenly, we heard someone shouting in Afrikaans, telling us to come out of the water immediately. We were around 11 to 13 years old at the time, and we were afraid. We thought about swimming away, but their voices grew louder, threatening us to get out of the water immediately. We all came out and stood on the shore, wet and scared, as we were marched towards the police station.

Arriving at the police station, we were taken into a room and told to stand in a straight line from the biggest to the smallest. They asked who can play the guitar. The policeman decided the one who plays the guitar should play, and the rest of us should sing. We sang with all our hearts, hoping it would help us get out of trouble. After we sang, one of the policemen came with a cane. He handed it to the biggest boy in the line and told him to hit the smallest boy. Fortunately, with my height, I was in the middle. The biggest boy, though large, did not have the heart to hit our friend. He lifted the cane and gently tapped the smallest boy.

The policemen, feeling mocked, then handed the cane to the smallest boy and told him to hit the biggest boy. They threatened him, saying if he didn't do it, they would hit him instead.

The small boy did exactly as he was told, bringing the cane down hard on the boy's buttocks. The big boy stood straight up and groaned with pain. The policemen felt entertained and laughed loudly seeing our friend groaning with pain, which entertained the policemen, who laughed loudly. Another policeman stood in front of us and harshly warned us never to swim in the bay again. Then they let us go. We left the police station in a hurry, our wet clothes no longer mattered; we

Chapter 1

were just relieved to get away. With our guitar, we all made our way straight home.

One day, sitting in the schoolyard with my friends, they taught me how to play guitar chords. I started to play when one of the older boys aggressively grabbed the guitar from me and started to play. He was always nasty and jealous whenever I played. His grabbing the guitar built resentment in me towards him. I looked at him, but what stopped me from fighting him was that he was much older and bigger than me. At that moment, a fight with him was out of the question.

Music and dance were the highlights in our neighbourhoods. As you walked past a house, you would often hear music playing. Music had the power to alter moods, change perceptions, and inspire change. Sitting with my friends, playing the guitar and singing, made us happy and helped us forget all the negativity around us. As time passed, drastic changes in my environment impacted me deeply. Gangs and gang wars emerged, bringing crime, drugs, domestic violence, and robbery. Being surrounded by these issues made for a difficult childhood. For some, alcohol and drugs became a refuge, and gambling escalated due to unemployment. These influences rapidly grew among the youth. Bullying, jealousy, envy, and even hatred started to manifest in the community. From Friday night through the weekend, I didn't have to see the trouble to know it was there; I could hear the domestic violence, shouting, screaming, and drunkenness in some homes. This way of life seemed normal, but feelings of helplessness and intimidation affected me. I wanted to do the right thing and not be influenced negatively, but instead, it sucked me in.

Entering high school, I did not take my education seriously. I often skipped school to go to the beach and swim in the bay, despite being previously warned by the police. Friends and fun were all that mattered to me. I reached a point where I had no interest in school, except for math, as I had a good teacher and enjoyed the subject. One day, while planning another fun day, I hid my math book in the bushes, intending to retrieve it the next day. However, it rained heavily that night, and my book was damaged and soaked. I was afraid, knowing I was in serious

SET FREE

trouble because all my written work was erased by the rain. This fear gave me more reason to continue skipping school. Despite knowing truancy was wrong, peer pressure prevailed.

I did not realise the importance of school. Instead, smoking, the beach, and fun seemed like the best choices. The school principal notified my parents about my truancy. My mother was disappointed and tried talking to me, but I told her I didn't want to go to school anymore. In South Africa, the education law required every school-aged child to attend school. However, influence, stubbornness, and rebellion were factors contributing to my disinterest in school. My mother often talked to me about the importance of education, but I was defiant and ignored her advice. Ignoring her gave me a sense of power, making me feel in control. I became tired of these conversations and wanted to do what I wanted. At the time, I didn't consider whether my choices were good or bad; I just didn't want to miss out on the fun with my friends.

Continuing to be obstinate, rebellious, and truant, I was not aware I was being observed, and steps were being taken to address my behaviour. The school notified the community social worker, who informed my parents and requested a visit to discuss my situation. One day, as I was riding my bike towards my house, a car drove past me. The lady driving the car looked up at me and smiled before stopping at my house. My mother had already informed me that the social worker was coming to visit, and I needed to be home, not with my friends.

I entered the lounge, and the lady was seated on the couch, smiling at me. She had a pen and folder in her hand, waiting for me. Her simple attire— a long skirt and flat brown sandals— complemented her warm personality and approach. I felt at ease talking to her. She was not loud or angry and did not scream at me. In a soft tone, she mentioned the importance of school and then listened attentively and patiently to what I had to say. I told her I would like to go to the Reformatory School of Industries, as I had heard it was a good school for someone like me.

There had been talk about this place amongst my friends. They spoke about a place called Ottery, a reformatory for boys where they trained physically, became fit, disciplined, educated, and learned a

Chapter 1

trade. It sounded good to me, and I was very interested. She looked at me and gently said, "Brian, you have two options: go back to school or go to reformatory. You choose." I liked my friends but realised my current situation— going back to school, which I found boring, was not the best option. I was always in trouble at home and at school, so maybe something different would help me do better and be a better person. I looked at the social worker and told her I wanted to go to the reformatory. She nodded, smiling, and said she would work on it. She wrote some notes in her book and left.

A few days later, my parents received a letter stating that they needed to appear in court with me. On arrival at the court, we were taken into a room where an officer sat behind a desk. After a discussion, he told me to wait outside of the room. I was not aware someone was outside waiting to escort me to the grill yards. I felt uneasy, anxious, and wondered what they were discussing about me. Suddenly, a policeman dressed in uniform appeared, approached me, and told me to follow him. I tried to indicate that I was waiting for my parents, who were in the room, but he was unconcerned and abruptly told me to come with him. I wanted to see my parents and did not get to say goodbye.

Following him, he took me to the grill yard, a place where prisoners would be waiting for court or be escorted to another prison. Some of the prisoners were tall, burly, and intimidating. I felt scared and so afraid. Fortunately, I saw two familiar faces—boys who lived in the same suburb as me. I walked towards them, and we started to talk. I found out we were all heading for the same place, called the Place of Safety, where boys going to the reformatory would wait until their paperwork was completed. This place was not far from my home. The locals described it as "just on top of the hill," overlooking the seaside called Treasure Beach.

The Place of Safety was a secured facility with high fences and gates around the property. While waiting there, my documents were being processed for reformatory school, and arrangements were being made to purchase my ticket to Cape Town, with two men assigned to escort me. At the facility, girls were separated from boys, and there were

SET FREE

dormitories but no school or chores. We were allowed to smoke, play games, and hang around all day. It was the same routine every day, and I quickly became bored. Deciding to escape, I jumped the high fence and ran all the way home. Surprisingly, nobody questioned me the way I had expected; they barely took note of my presence. Perhaps they were tired of my inability to settle down. Feeling disappointed, I returned to the Place of Safety, determined to go to reformatory school.

I received a letter from a friend who was already at the reformatory. He assured me not to worry and that everything would be okay. The social worker visited me at the Place of Safety to inform me that all the paperwork had been finalised and my departure date for the reformatory had been confirmed. She offered me the option to either stay at the Place of Safety or go home to spend my last few days with my family. I chose to go home.

A very painful memory always stayed with me. I reflected on a close family member who tried to discipline me during a particularly rebellious period of my life. He took me to his house, away from my friends and parents. One night, while I was fast asleep in just my pyjama pants, I was abruptly woken up and told to lie on the couch on my stomach. Confused but respecting him as an elder, I did as instructed. Suddenly, I felt a sharp sting and burn on my bare back—a lash from a whip. I jumped up in fright, but a second lash followed. The pain was intense. Disoriented, I ran towards the door, but it was locked, and the key was removed. Frantically, I tried other doors, but they were all locked. Overpowered by another family member, I was held down and repeatedly whipped.

The first opportunity I had to escape, I ran all the way home, in pain, my back feeling like it was on fire. My mother noticed the marks and was highly upset. She confronted the family member about how he could use a whip on me. This incident left me with lasting feelings of fear and anxiety, especially towards that family member. I yearned for a change and to escape from it all. Deep in thought, the screeching of the train coming to a halt brought me back to my senses.

Chapter 1

We were finally stopping, coming to the end of my journey—a long three-day train ride. There was so much I had reflected on, the good and the bad. I thought this was it, but then the escort explained we had just one more train to take, and it would go straight to the reformatory. I felt worn out and tired.

Stepping off the train, with an escort on either side of me, we walked towards the next stationed train, leaving soon. Stepping onto this train, I noticed there were no coaches. I figured it out—this would not be a long trip. The train started and we were on our way, passing a lot of suburbs. Soon, the train stopped.

Chapter 2
Reformatory

Stepping off the train, I looked around and saw no buildings in sight. I wondered what the next form of transport would be—a bus or a boat? All I could see was a massive forest ahead of us, with very tall trees. I had never seen so many trees clumped together. We walked amid the tall red gum trees, with escorts on either side of me, informing me we were now going for a very long walk. It felt like a five-minute walk, with no talking; all I could hear was the crunching of dry leaves underfoot. In the distance, I saw buildings ahead of me. As we got closer, I saw rooms that looked like offices. I turned and was surprised to see a familiar face waving and smiling at me. I recognised my friend from Durban and thought to myself, there must be more Durban boys here.

My escorts checked me in at the main office, did the necessary paperwork, and signed me in. The officer attending to me looked stern and cheekily explained that the carpentry trade I was interested in was not available. I would have to wait at the tailors until the carpentry trade became available. The trades offered were electrician, tailoring, mechanics, plumbing, upholstery, carpentry, building, and shoemaking. The school was divided into two groups, housing 500 boys: A and B Group.

When the A group attended school, the B Group would be learning a trade in the workshop. The reformatory was divided into three sections, each with a hostel: Alpha, Gamma, and Beta. Each group

Chapter 2

was identified by colours. The Alpha Group was for the smaller boys, wearing blue belts on their uniforms. The Gamma Group was for the medium-age group, wearing yellow belts. The Beta Group was for the big boys, wearing red belts. These groups wore uniforms consisting of a khaki short-sleeve buttoned shirt and khaki short pants. In winter, you were given a thin navy-blue jersey. You received one pair of shoes per year; if you lost your shoes, you would go barefoot for the rest of the year.

My clothing was handed to me, coded with a number as a form of identification. My number was 3845, which made me feel like a prisoner in a jail. Later, I learned this number sometimes took the place of my name, especially when I received mail from my parents. Before I got my mail, it would be opened and read, then handed to me. If I wrote a letter to my parents, the letter would be handed to the officer in an envelope, which was not allowed to be sealed so he could read it first, seal it, and then mail it to my parents. Every letter coming in or going out had to have my number on the envelope to identify me. The hostel buildings were colour-coded as well.

The colours red, blue, and yellow identified each hostel and the age group. The officer continued talking, explaining that every boy arriving at the reformatory would start in the Alpha group. For now, I would be there for one month, assessed by my age, physical appearance, size, and body structure. The officer looked at me and said harshly, "There is also a Delta Prison for runaways, committing crimes, drug offences, and any violence," pointing at me. "Don't even try anything because that is where you will be headed."

He continued, "The gates are always open; they are never closed. If you try to escape, you will get caught and punished." He spoke in Afrikaans, saying, "We are now your mother and father. Here, you will do as you are told, listen to us, and follow instructions." He mentioned with an attitude that they were in control. Mr. V was the officer's name. He addressed me in English but could speak Afrikaans. These were the two most common languages spoken in the reformatory. I was

SET FREE

English-speaking but familiar with Afrikaans, as my mother spoke it to me and my siblings at home. Coming from the Northern Cape, my mother's first language was Afrikaans.

The Delta prisoners wore a uniform: a blue shirt, khaki shorts, and a thin brown jersey for winter. Every hostel was made up dormitories, with two prefects in charge of each dormitory. The prefects' duties included keeping the dormitories clean and maintained in good condition. Soon, I would find out what "clean and good condition" meant.

Whilst Mr V spoke to me, he looked at my finger, he noticed the ring on my finger. He said, "No rings allowed here, so you need to get the ring off your finger." I tried to tell him I couldn't get it off because it was stuck. His look alone told me I had to sort it out immediately. Mr. V told me to change into my uniform, and then I would be taken to the tailor's. Some boys approached me and commented about the ring. "We could help you get the ring off; it's not allowed here." I sensed they had other intentions and wanted the ring.

The ring was all they wanted. One of the guys walked towards me with scissors, held my finger, and cut the ring off. The ring fell onto the floor, and they all dived towards it, trying to grab it. I quickly said, "No problem. If you take the ring, the officer will inquire, and I'll tell him you guys have it." Immediately, they handed the ring back to me, knowing the punishment would be severe. This was my first dramatic episode at the reformatory.

I started to settle into the routine. The prefects were in charge of my hostel. At 5 pm, we took a compulsory shower, which was strictly supervised. In one room, I would undress and then move into a bigger room with around 20 showers along the wall. There was only one tap to open and shut all the showers, which is why shower time was supervised. The other five dormitories stood outside in a line, waiting for their turn.

Come rain, storm, summer, or winter, a cold shower was all we got year-round. In the showers, talking was not allowed. We would enter the room, undress, and stand naked in the shower, waiting for the

Chapter 2

tap to open. Everyone had to be under the shower at the same time. The tap would open with a gush of cold water for a few seconds, just enough to wet our bodies. Once wet, the next step was to soap ourselves and wait.

Approximately 20 boys had to be checked by the supervisor to ensure each one of us was properly soaped before he could continue to open the tap. If one of us was not soaped properly, then we would have to wait longer until he was satisfied. The worst was yet to come: as we stood there with soap drying on our bodies, we began to shiver from the cold. Once the last boy was soaped and ready, the tap would open again for just a few seconds, giving us time to rinse off. We had to be quick because once the tap shut off, it stayed off. This was the shower procedure.

Sometimes, boys would inadvertently talk to each other while drying off in the dressing room. If caught, they would feel the stick on their naked bodies. After dressing, we were allowed a little social time with our friends until the hooter signalled supper at 6 p.m. We would line up outside the big dining room, which had long tables seating eight boys, four on either side. There were no porcelain, chinaware, or glassware—only steel bowls, cups, and spoons.

The prefect would escort us to the dining table group by group, ensuring the chairs were filled row by row. The person in charge would then instruct us to sit up straight, be quiet, and pray. I learned the hard way to guard my food during grace; otherwise, it would vanish, especially sausages. During grace, one hand would cover my plate while the other covered my face, peeking through my fingers. Not protecting your supper meant it could disappear right before your eyes. Talking was not allowed while eating.

My time there was not very long when an incident happened in the dining hall. A head prefect from the Beta hostel, a big, well-built, older boy, tried to assert his authority. My friend spoke to me, and I answered softly. The prefect saw and headed towards me, kicking me in the mouth. I tried to block but he got me. Anger swirled in me. I tackled him, grabbed him, and pushed him against the wall. My mouth was

SET FREE

bleeding, and we started to scuffle on the floor. The person in charge commanded us to stop. Continuing to fight with a prefect would result in immediate punishment. Hitting a prefect was a serious offence, but to me, kicking me in the mouth was unacceptable.

Every morning, still asleep, the lights would be switched on, signalling it was time to wake up. We washed our faces, brushed our teeth, and performed duties and chores as instructed by the prefects. We were then split into our groups. When the hooter went off, everyone had to assemble in front of the linen room, standing row by row.

The supervisor in charge of each hostel would address the boys. Names and numbers would be called out for the boys to collect their mail. This time was also used for the attendance register. The prefect would do a roll call. Once the roll call was finished, the prefect would command, "Attention, stand at ease, left right, left right." We were marched like soldiers all the way to the dining hall for breakfast. Breakfast consisted of jungle oats (a porridge), rooibos tea, two slices of peanut butter and jam, and sometimes a boiled egg.

The best hair brushes the boys used, including myself, were made from a lady's curler or roller. The curler would be cut with scissors to make it flat. We kept this hairbrush in our pockets all day, using it whenever we needed to brush our hair or tidy up. Shoes were taken very good care of, with a process involving shoe polish, water, a stocking, and a cloth. Applying the polish with a cloth around the finger was done with time, pride, and care because the finishing touch was a shining shoe that looked brand new.

Nivea creme was used for our skin and Vaseline for both hair and skin. During the winter, Cape Town would be so cold. Our thin jerseys did not keep out the cold or help in any way. Instead, we would sneak out our oranges after dinner and rub the segments of the orange into our jersey to cover the holes and to keep the cold out. Due to my built and structure, I was transferred to the Beta Hostel (the big boys). Naturally, if boys came from the same area, they would form a clique, feeling comfortable because of similar traits. Coming from Durban, we were called the Durban boys. There were also the Cape Town boys

Chapter 2

and the Johannesburg boys. Different groups were formed amongst the boys.

Durban boys had a special place; they would gather outside the workshop. One Sunday morning before breakfast, during a small social break, a gang fight broke out with the leader of the Cape Town group. He had approached a Durban boy who was sitting with us and threatened him with harsh words. The Durban boy mumbled a few words, then suddenly stood up and kicked the Cape Town leader off his feet.

Sensing the tension in the air, we knew this was serious trouble. Standing up, the Durban boys (including myself) ran towards the shed. The shed stored garden tools such as spades, hoes, slashers (bush knives), and big garden forks. A Durban boy worked in the shed, and when we ran into the shed, he distributed the tools to us. I was running with the Durban boys, garden tools in our hands, chasing the Cape Town boys. It was hard to determine who was who, as everyone wore the same uniform. The Cape Town boys ran towards the hospital on the reformatory premises. Their leader grabbed the hospital attendant, screaming that the Durban boys wanted to kill him. The Durban boys retreated, returned all the gardening tools to the shed, and made our way to our special spot where we always gathered.

We started to talk amongst ourselves when suddenly, in the distance, another gang of boys approached us. As they came closer, we realised they were the Johannesburg boys. They told us they had heard about the fight and that next time, they would be willing to stand with us should another fight break out.

Remaining in the reformatory for a certain period qualified one to go out and work in the community, in a residential area. On Saturday mornings, all those eligible to work for the locals would assemble in the school courtyard. The man in charge would call our names out, and sometimes two boys would go out to work for one family. Attempting to escape was unacceptable and would definitely result in punishment, as well as being barred from working in the community.

I would cut a vast area of grass with a slasher (not an electric lawnmower) using my hands to manually cut the lawn. By the end of the

SET FREE

day, my palms would be covered with painful blisters. A day's work included weeding, trimming, watering plants, cleaning windows, and sweeping. For all this work, I would earn forty cents (40c) a day. There was a tuck shop on the reformatory premises where I would spend my earnings on items like Oroz juice, soap, sweet aid, biscuits, cigarettes, toothpaste, etc.

With my forty cents, I could only choose two items. My friend and I, who shared the same dormitory and locker, would make deals to share our purchases. For example, if I bought toothpaste and soap, he would buy Oroz juice and biscuits. We always made sure to have a bar of soap each for shower time. Dinner was served early, and by bedtime, I would still feel hungry. Biscuits were our favourite bedtime snack.

Eating these snacks was quite a process. Making sure nobody was looking, I would remove the biscuits from my locker and place them under my pillow. As soon as the lights went out and the boys in the dormitory were settled in their beds, it was snack time. Opening the biscuits quietly was challenging, so I did it under the blankets to muffle the sound. I would take a few out and pass them to my friend next to me.

We would eat the biscuits under the blanket to avoid any chewing sounds being heard by the rest of the boys. If we were caught or reported eating biscuits, there were consequences, and we would be forced to share. The reporter would be very observant, knowing exactly what was happening at night. He would slide on his belly under all the beds, heading towards ours. As soon as we passed the biscuits, his head would pop up between our beds. We had no option but to give him a handful of biscuits to keep him quiet. If we didn't, we would be in serious trouble.

I had been at Ottery for about two months when I gave up cigarettes. One of the boys challenged us to see who could give up smoking the longest. I took up the challenge. That same day, we had to queue up in the dining hall, where smoking was not allowed. A prefect I knew walked up to me and handed me a lit cigarette. Without thinking, I took it and pulled on it twice.

Chapter 2

Only after I had taken a few pulls on the cigarette did it dawn on me that I was supposed to have given it up. A guy standing next to me asked for it, but I was so angry with myself that instead of passing the cigarette to him, I threw it on the floor and stomped it out. This was the last time I smoked a cigarette. Now, I am thankful to GOD and to the guy who put the challenge forward. Since that day, I have never smoked or desired to smoke, and this helped me give up a bad habit forever.

Cultivating the land was another task we had to perform. Since one group would be at school and the other at trade school, if one of the teachers was absent, we would have to go and cultivate the land. The area was vast, and in the summer, we would work in intense heat with the sun beating down on us. In winter, it was freezing, working in a wide-open space under the sky with only a thin jersey, no warm jackets, boots, or clothes to keep me warm. We worked in our reformatory uniforms. Cultivating was done manually; there was no machinery to make things easy for us. We used our physical strength and garden tools—hoes, rakes, and spades—to till the ground, prepare the soil, and create furrows to plant our fruits and vegetables.

The sequence to cultivate a vast area involved fifteen boys standing in a line side by side. Each one held a spade, facing his back to the vast area. The boy on the left would dig a hole, casting the soil to the left, leaving an empty hole in front of him. The boy to the right would do the same, casting his soil to the boy on the left. When the vegetables had grown, we would pick them and use them for cooking in the reformatory.

This was hard work. Individual traits like discipline, perseverance, and a strong work ethic were essential. We worked under strict supervision, often from a man who also supervised prisoners in Delta. It was difficult, and we had no option but to follow instructions. Rain, sun, heat, cold, blisters, pain—we worked through it all. No one was there to comfort us, give us a pain tablet, ask how we felt, or check if we could manage; it was all about the work. The Afrikaner supervisors came across as cruel, hard, cold, heartless, and steadfast. The reformatory was like a prison, and the same rules applied when cutting down the tall red gum trees.

If a teacher was absent at school or in the workshop, a group of us would be taken outdoors amongst the trees. The first step was to tie the rope at the top of the tree, and then we would have to manually chop the bottom to weaken it. The person in charge would stand there watching us, whip in hand, loudly saying, "Trek" (meaning pull). We would pull, and the tree would bend. He would say "Trek" again, and the cracking sound of the tree indicated it was coming down.

Once this happened, the next step was to run as fast as we could from the falling tree. Sometimes, if we let go too early, the tree would spring back, and we would be shouted at and whipped. These trees could grow up to twenty meters high. The same supervisor who worked with the jail boys also supervised us cutting down the gum trees. He was rough and harsh, showing no compassion towards us. After the trees fell, they were left to dry for a few days. We then had to chop them into logs using a hand saw, with no gloves to protect our hands, which were often blistered from previous work. The logs were used for firewood for cooking, as our food was cooked with steam.

One day would be a school day, and the next would be a trade day. If a teacher was not available on any of these days, the supervisor of the Delta Prison would sort us out. There was an old, red, brick, broken-down building with a pile of bricks. We would sit out there all day, smashing bricks with a hammer.

The dormitories were huge, with tiled wooden floors that we had to keep clean by washing, polishing, and shining them. After applying the polish with a cloth, we had to shine the floors. Three rows of six boys, including myself, would kneel side by side, leaning forward and holding polish brushes in both hands. One of the boys would lead a song in rhythm, creating a beat like rhythmic activity to motivate us to get the job done. The song would go as follows: "One two, two to one, eh ah, one two, two to one, eh ah." We would crawl backward on our knees to the end of the dormitory floor, then crawl forward, still repeating the song, to shine the floor ahead of us. If the leader knew we were

Chapter 2

going to have nuts for dinner, he would say, "Is doppies vanaand, eh ah" (meaning "It's nuts tonight" in English). This motion was repeated many times, moving the brush from left to right, until the floors were shining and the prefect was satisfied.

Attending school, I continued with math as a subject. The teacher was strict but comical and explained math lessons very well. During the lesson, he would randomly ask questions related to the topic to see if we were paying attention. If we failed to give the right answer, he would say, "Stretch your arms out like a bird." With arms still stretched, he would then hit us towards our ribs with a stick. Familiar with his tactics, some boys would raise one arm as he approached with the stick. He would then say, "A bird cannot fly with one wing."

The gym trainer was very strict and believed in being one hundred percent practical. The gym room had two benches parallel to each other. We would sit on the benches facing each other, placing our feet under the bench and hands behind our heads. We had to lean back until the back of our heads were just a few millimetres away from the ground. Before touching the ground, we had to lift ourselves towards our feet. Sometimes, midway through, the trainer would tell us to go down again. There would be no break, and this would go on for approximately fifteen times or more, depending on when the trainer said to stop. We would be punished if we did not carry out the training. It often felt very strenuous, but we had no choice but to heed the trainer's instructions.

When the trainer decided there would be no gym session, we had swimming lessons instead. At home, there were no local swimming pools, so we would go to the beach, which was just over the hill. In the reformatory, swimming was done in a pool. A class of boys, including myself, would be taken to the swimming pool. Upon arrival, we would be given swimwear and instructed to jump in and swim. Whilst swimming, we would be called out of the pool and instructed to line up and make our way to the low diving board, taking turns to dive.

There were two boards: a high diving board and a low one. When it was my turn, I would jump on the board, look down, stand for a while, and then jump feet first, confident because I knew I could swim. The trainer would then instruct us to return to the board and this time, dive headfirst by thrusting our bodies forward. I was worried because I was not familiar with diving in this manner.

I had dived with a big splash (a belly flop, as they would call it). If the instructor was not satisfied with my dive, he would want me to dive again. I would hear the words, "Line up again, but this time, everyone make their way to the high diving boards." Fear gripped me, as I had never done this before. My hands would start to tremble as I made my way up the stairs to the high diving board. I could hear the boys mumbling amongst themselves. I whispered to one of the boys, "I am scared. I have never done this before." The boy said, "You have to do it. There is no option; the instructor will make you do it." For me, it felt like a point of no return. I had to find my way up to the high diving board. I was being forced, and there was nothing I could do or say but go ahead.

I made my way towards the tip of the board, which was shaky. The board would move up and down. Procrastinating thoughts would rise in my head: should I turn around and face the consequences or should I jump? Turning around, I saw the instructor making his way towards the steps of the high diving board. Oh gosh! He was coming for me. Looking towards the water, terrified, I could see the tiles; the water was clear. I knew I would hit the tiles.

By now, the instructor was very close to the steps. Hearing him closer, I jumped in a second, making sure my legs would touch the ground first. Before I knew it, I was swimming out. Phew! I had done it; I had jumped off the high diving board. It sounded and seemed cruel. Days later, a somersault dive meant nothing to me. I had overcome my fear, gained confidence, and brought out the best in me. I began to look forward to swimming lessons. The reformatory made me a good, confident swimmer.

Chapter 3
Holidays (1973)

Fourteen months had passed, and I was homesick and missed my family. A special requirement needed to be followed for me to go home for the June holidays. The social worker had to visit my home to see if there was a bed available for me to sleep on. A written letter would be sent to the reformatory confirming the social worker had been to my home and that the necessary requirement was met. A good behaviour report was also needed to permit me to go on holiday. Train fare would be sent from my parents. All these requirements had to be met; otherwise, I would be unable to go home.

My name would be displayed on the notice board at the main office. Daily, I would have to check. My name would be on the board if all the criteria were met. I started to become anxious, until one day I walked to the notice board to check, and there they were—all the ticks next to my name and number. Phew! I would be going home.

Back on the train for the three-day journey home, I was filled with excitement and happiness. The train sped along, and I couldn't wait to see my family, friends, and my home sweet home. Upon arrival, my family was overjoyed to see me, though I felt very tired from the long journey. Three days of my holiday had been spent traveling, but it was such a good feeling to see everyone again and just be home. What a relief!

SET FREE

The next day, my mother took me into the city to do some clothing shopping. She bought me fashionable shoes called Crockett and Jones. Over the following days, I had plenty of stories to share with my parents and siblings, who listened attentively since these were real-life experiences. My hard work in the reformatory had paid off. Cleaning, polishing, and shining the floors at home was not new to me. The house felt smaller inside and out. Cutting the grass and weeding the garden for my parents was not difficult at all; it was my pleasure, and I enjoyed doing it. My family was really surprised to see me working and doing all the chores. My mother, smiling, would tell the neighbours, "Is this really our Brian?"

I noticed many changes had taken place during my absence. My friends seemed more grown up, some with different outlooks on life. My family continued to fuss over me, giving me a good time, as they had missed me too. I spent time with my friends, who told me about a group of people at the school hall from another city. The school hall was always available to accommodate holiday groups arriving by bus and staying on the premises. My friends and I decided to go meet these people, make friends, and socialise. The school was not far from my home, so we walked over there, and I wore my new shoes.

Speaking of shoes, I had lost my shoes in the reformatory and had been barefoot for the next six months. In winter, my feet would freeze, and walking on gravel was not easy. I had developed a thick layer of skin on the soles of my feet. My mother had noticed this since I had come home for the holidays.

We walked into the hall and greeted the group. Whilst sitting on chairs, a few boys I knew walked in. I recall one of them had bullied me before. At the time, I couldn't fight back because he seemed older and stronger than me. This was the same guy who would snatch the guitar from me whenever I tried to play it. He recognised me, and his biggest mistake was to walk past and tramp on my new shoes. In the reformatory, we cleaned our shoes with pride and joy. They had to look clean and new. By trampling on my shoes, I figured he was sending a message that he was not scared of me despite my time in the reformatory.

Chapter 3

Thinking it could have been a mistake, I looked at him and said, "You tramped on me." I expected an apology, but instead, he said, "Do you want me to do it again?" I stood up and looked him square in the eye, saying, "You won't do it again." He replied, "So what are you going to do about it?" I answered, "I can do something about it right now, right here."

My best friend, who was with me, was a rough character and always carried a knife. The bully suggested we go outside, and as we were making our way out, my friend asked if he could take him on, eager for a fight. I told him no, I would handle it myself. Today was the day; it was payback time. All I could think about was revenge. We all walked towards a building around the corner, near the caretakers' living quarters. I started to shape up, and we faced each other, letting go of a few punches. I made sure he wouldn't get a chance; I gave him punch after punch. He knew he was in trouble and leaped towards me, holding me tight around my waist. He hadn't expected it to be this hard for him. I realised fear had gripped him, and his friends pleaded with me to let him go.

Hearing noises from around the corner, the caretakers arrived to see what was all the commotion about. I was familiar with the surroundings, as this was where I went to school in my early years at Northgate Primary. The caretakers had remembered me and were surprised to see me, asking where I had been all this time since they had not seen me for a long time. I ended up letting him go. He had spread rumours that he had been drunk during the fight and made excuses for not being able to fight me. When I heard about this, I was not happy and decided to confront him again. I found him, demanded answers, and asked him what he was going to do about it. We needed to finish this.

Raising my hand, I placed my palm on his chest, smacking and pushing him. Repeatedly, I asked, "What are you going to do about it?" His friends started to beg, "Brian, leave him alone, please, Brian, please." Feeling satisfied and finally in control, I let him go.

I continued to enjoy the holidays with my family and friends. At night, as I lay on my bed, thoughts ran through my head. Questions like,

SET FREE

would I go back to the reformatory? It felt so good to be back home, but I knew there would be consequences if I didn't return. It would seem like I was a runaway. There was no option; I had to return to the reformatory. My mind was made up.

Six months later, I returned home for my second holidays, in December, just in time for Christmas. I was so excited to be back home again and see my family. My mother took me to the Northern Cape, Vryburg, to see my grandmother (my ouma), whom I loved dearly. She was so sweet, loving, and caring. I was happy to see everyone, and they were happy too. My mum's way of celebrating special occasions involved buying a live sheep from the local farmers. My uncle and cousins were good at slaughtering, cleaning, and preparing the sheep for the pot. My aunties would get the fire ready and start the cooking.

Instruments like the saxophone, guitar, and keyboard could be heard in the house. Some of my cousins were skilled musicians. I enjoyed the music, the plentiful food, and the great family time with my cousins, aunties, uncles, my mum, and grandmother. It was a good time to catch up. After holidaying in the Northern Cape, I returned to Durban to my home. I stayed there for the rest of the holiday period. Soon, I would be returning to the reformatory. Mixed emotions swirled within me, knowing there was one more year, and at the same time, not knowing what lay ahead.

I told myself, no more fights. I would have to try hard, very hard, this year and not get into any trouble. Getting into trouble would jeopardise my chances of leaving the reformatory for good. I might have to stay there longer. I remembered the time I got into a fight with a reformatory boy. He came to me and said, "Brian, I would like to box with you." I replied, "No wrestling, only boxing." This was an agreement we both reached. We started to box, and he noticed I was getting the upper hand.

Suddenly, something came over him, and he lifted me up and threw me onto the tarmac road. I did not expect him to do this; he took me by surprise. Ending up with bruises on my shoulder and head, I got angry

Chapter 3

and disappointed. He did not keep his word. Remembering there were bricks behind the builder's workshop, I ran there, angry, grabbed a brick, and smashed it into the ground, breaking it in two halves. I held one half in my left hand and the other in my right hand. The reason for this was that if he ducked the first half, I would get him with the second. Exactly what I thought happened. He ducked the first half, and while ducking, I threw the second half, hitting him on his shoulder and head. Some boys came by and stopped us from fighting. The holidays were over, and I journeyed back to the reformatory, telling myself one more year and I needed to behave and stay out of trouble.

On a cold winter morning, we were woken up by the prefect in charge. He split us into two groups. The first group remained indoors doing dormitory chores. The second group did chores outdoors. A vast area outdoors needed cleaning, raking, and picking up leaves with our bare hands (no gloves). The morning frost on my fingers and hands would turn blue, aching with cold (frost bite). The prefect who supervised made sure we carried out our chores as instructed. Somehow, for no reason, he started to load chore after chore on me. I began to think in my head, was he being deliberate? Did he know it was nearing my time to leave? Was he trying to set me up, stir trouble, and get me punished so I would remain longer in the reformatory? He had developed a nasty attitude towards me and would bully me. My thoughts were confirmed, and feelings of resentment started to build up in me. I felt angry and upset and called him out for a fight. I wanted a fair fight. Fighting with a prefect was big trouble. I tried so hard but could not tolerate the nastiness.

Tired of being pushed around, I felt anger build up inside of me. Today was the day I had enough. We started to box, and I got the better of him. The other boys came to stop us, and we both ceased fighting, returning to our chores. I didn't know the prefect had reported me for fighting with him. The report went to the person in charge of the hostel, who stood for no nonsense. The head prefect of our hostel, who came from the same city as me, was present at the discussion about the next steps to be taken since I fought with a prefect.

SET FREE

When it was parade time, I was called out by my number and taken to the linen room. All the prefects in charge would give me a good hiding. Fortunately, the head prefect, who was my friend, had my back and intervened, saying he would sort the problem out. My punishment was to be taken to my friend's dormitory, where he would implement hard labour to discipline me. The hooter blew, signalling us to assemble at the parade for breakfast. I was informed I would have to go to the older boys' dormitory.

That first night, my friend said, "Brian, in this dormitory, there is no going on your knees to clean floors. The whole idea is to have you here to relax and look forward to going home." I was so happy to hear this; what a relief.

Twice a week and on weekends, I worked for the workshops manager at his home. I did gardening chores, watered the flowers, cut the grass using a slasher, and raked and swept. Mr. K, an Englishman, managed all the workshop trades. I tried so hard throughout the year to stay out of trouble. My birthday was coming up, and in November 1974, I would be turning eighteen years old. December arrived, and my time had come to leave. I was going home for good. I had to go to the tailors to choose a suit and colour of my choice. The actual tailors were reformatory boys who chose tailoring as a trade. My choice of style and colour was pinstripes, a charcoal grey with turn-ups.

As my day of leaving the reformatory approached, at night I would lie on my bed, feeling excited. Finally, I was leaving after spending three years in that place. I wondered what my future would be like out there; thinking about it overwhelmed me. This place was like a prison. I remembered mornings when every dormitory of boys had to stand in rows in the courtyard while the supervisor addressed us. There had to be silence when he spoke. If he saw anyone talking, he would suddenly appear with a cane, whipping everyone on their legs, even the innocent boys. The prefects worked together with the supervisor; they knew if they ill-treated us, they would gain favour with him.

At night, there was a night watchman on duty, ensuring everyone was in their dormitories and watching out for any runaways. Once the

Chapter 3

dormitory lights were switched off, there had to be silence. If he heard any sound or talking, all the boys in the dormitory would have to come outside. We would stand in rows with our hands raised in the air. The prefects in the dormitory were not punished; they watched what happened to us. We would remain there, arms raised, for as long as the security felt necessary. It was tiring standing with arms raised, and if we became tired and our hands came down, we would be whipped with a stick. This punishment applied to even the innocent boys. I was so happy that it was finally time to go home, for good.

Chapter 4
Home For Good (1974)

The day had come; it was time to leave the reformatory for good. I shook hands with my friends and was given a new pair of khaki clothes and brand-new shoes to take home. I wore my tailored suit, feeling and looking smart, ready to go. A three-day journey lay ahead. The first stop was in Cape Town, where I boarded another train to Durban. This time, my stop was at Pietermaritzburg station. Stepping off the train, my two sisters and their husbands were there to meet me. We were all excited to see each other again.

I visited and stayed for a few hours in Pietermaritzburg at my sister's home. Then, my brother-in-law and my eldest sister drove me down to Durban. Finally, I was home—home sweet home. It felt unbelievable. My mother had informed me that, out of concern, she had already spoken to my uncle about a job for me. He visited our home and told me that next Wednesday, I would start a job working for the railway. My brother-in-law, my sister's husband, was willing to teach me a welding trade.

I would walk to my sister's house, down in the valley, where my brother-in-law would give me welding lessons in the evenings after work. On a Sunday afternoon, my brother-in-law visited my home and said he had a welding job ready for me to start. My mother was not happy because she preferred me to start a job with my uncle, who had offered first. My brother-in-law could see I was in a tough spot and mentioned that it was up to me to decide.

Chapter 4

If I decided to take the welding job, I would have to be at his house early Monday morning. If I chose my uncle's railway job, I would start on Wednesday. Decisions, decisions—it was so hard to choose. I didn't want to cause any ill feelings among my family. I wanted to please my mother and not make her feel I was letting her down. I wanted her to be happy. I weighed both jobs, asking myself which one would be better for my future.

I spoke to my mother, saying, "On Monday, I will go to my brother-in-law's job. If I am unsuccessful, I will take my uncle's job with the railway." Even though I was taking the step to pursue the welding job, I did not feel confident. I wasn't sure of myself since I had only been practicing welding with my brother-in-law for a short time. To qualify for the welding job, I would be required to pass a welding test.

On Monday morning, I arrived at the gate of the welding company. The recruiting foreman came out, called my name, and took me to the office to sign me on. Then, we headed to the welding school. This was my first experience in the real working world. I was nervous, and everything around me felt new and intimidating. I was given a chance to do a practice run before starting the actual welding test. Fortunately, my brother-in-law was there to instruct and guide me.

Nervously, I attempted the welding test. My weld had to be tested on a bending machine to determine if I had succeeded. I watched as my welded piece was bent on the machine. Pressure was applied, and I started feeling anxious as it bent and bent until I heard a loud CRACK! No, this couldn't be happening. My world stood still for a moment. The guy who tested my weld said, "Continue working; we will chat soon."

I noticed a sentence a previous welder had written on a plate: "Heartbreaker, my family depends on you." This was serious stuff. Men would go home without a job if their weld test failed. Feeling disappointed in myself, I continued working. The foreman then called me to dismiss me along with the others who had been unsuccessful. I walked out with my head down, but as I looked up, I saw my brother-in-law walking towards me. He said, "Brian, go back to the job. I am going to

SET FREE

arrange for a retest." I thought I would slip out quietly and call it a day, but my brother-in-law's support gave me a second chance.

I was told to continue practicing, and when I felt confident and ready, I could attempt the weld test again. The second time around, I passed. I did it, thanks to my brother-in-law for taking the time to teach me, supporting me, not giving up on me, and giving me a second attempt at my first weld test. The feeling was good, but I knew there was still a lot to learn about welding. Passing this test motivated me to learn more. The money was good, and I was so happy.

My first welding job was the Mike G. Rutherford Oil Rig for the Gulf of Mexico, being built at Dorbyl Durban, South Africa. My trade in the reformatory was carpentry, and here I was doing welding on an oil rig. I seized every opportunity to learn and gain experience, not letting any knowledge related to my new trade pass me by. Daily at work, I thoroughly enjoyed learning new welding techniques. I loved this trade and continued in the job, earning a good wage as a welder.

Encouraging me, my brother-in-law said to me, "Brian, you need to open a savings account with a bank." The bank would provide me with a bank book, allowing me to watch my money grow every time I made a deposit. I continued to save until I reached a point where I could purchase a car. I spoke to my mother and father, letting them know I intended to buy a car. They both accompanied me to go car shopping.

At the car sale, a seven-seater, cherry red Chev Constantia 1973 model with a black hard top caught my eye. My parents suggested other cars, but my mind was made up—I liked the Chevy. I had to organise with one of my friends who had a driver's licence to pick up my car for me, as I didn't have a licence at the time. Nothing mattered but my new car. Buying a car made me feel good; I had achieved something. I was so excited that I built a garage for my car, using asbestos for the roof and wooden poles.

A Christian friend I worked with offered to teach me how to drive my new car. He took me home in the morning after our night shift, drove the car out of the garage, and parked it in the lane. He told me to jump in on the driver's side. Feeling nervous, I told him I couldn't drive. He

Chapter 4

insisted, telling me it was an automatic car and I would only need to use one foot.

I jumped in, and he showed me the ignition, indicators, handbrakes, brakes, and how to hold the steering wheel, explaining how everything worked in the car. Nervous but determined, I put the key in the ignition, turned it, and the car started. I placed my foot on the gas pedal, and the car moved forward. I was finally driving the car up the lane and onto the road. I drove to the top of the hill and back home. He also explained the rules of the road and staying in my lane. As I continued to drive, I became more confident, which gave me the courage to take the driving test and legally obtain my driver's licence. His lessons helped me and still stay with me today.

On weekdays, I would use my car to go to work. On weekends, it was party time with my friends. Confidence and self-esteem kicked in, and I truly felt like I was the man. Cleaning my car was done with pride and joy, giving me a sense of satisfaction. I used rally car polish along with a fresh fragrance, and the tyres would be polished. Transportation was no longer a problem. I had worked for Dorbyl for almost a year.

One weekend, my friend and I decided to go to a dance at the city hall in town. I used my car. A band from our district was going to play music at the dance. When we arrived, we walked in and stood in the passage, having a general conversation. Three young guys from our district approached us and mentioned that there was a gang leader with his guys who had told one of them to stab someone. Whilst we were still talking, this gang leader came right in front of me and said, "Stab them." I looked him in the face and, with no fear, said, "There is no one stabbing anyone here."

He turned to his guys and indicated they should walk away, probably not knowing if I had a weapon on me. I asked my friend if he had a weapon in case I needed it, and he handed one to me. Not long after, I heard a commotion—the guys who walked away had attacked the guys from my district. Feeling obligated to help, I approached the gang leader and his group and attacked them. Suddenly, a fight broke out. I was stabbed in my hand while trying to block with my arm. I felt a burn

SET FREE

on my shoulder and realised I had been stabbed there too. Looking around, I noticed I was all alone. I tried to walk towards a wall to see from which angle they were coming. There was a passage nearby, and one of the guys came from behind and stabbed me in the back, very close to my spine (as I later found out at the hospital). Bleeding, I chased the guy into the passage but stopped, realising it could be a trap. I came back into the hall and entered the private bar.

People were sitting on chairs around tables, having their drinks in the bar. I knew now the war was raging and I would have to fend for myself. Bleeding profusely, I knew I was being attacked. I jumped over the bar counter, grabbing empty bottles and throwing them one by one towards the entrance of the bar. People began to scatter and ran out screaming. I didn't want those guys to enter the bar. When the empty bottles were all gone, I started to go for the full bottles on the shelf. The sound of breaking glass continued, and I realised the bar was empty; everybody had left out of fear. I was all alone behind the counter. I jumped over the counter again, this time with two bottles in my hand. I smashed them on the floor, carrying the broken pieces in my hands, and rushed into the hall where people were dancing. Every time I attempted to go into the crowd, wanting to see where these guys were, the crowd screamed and opened up. Seeing the exit sign, I threw the broken bottles down, trying to make my way out.

Whilst walking out, I noticed a guy with his arm around a girl and a knife in his hand. He had told her he was going to stab me, not knowing this girl knew me (I got to know this later because she told me). She looked, and seeing it was me, she said, "Brian, look out, this guy wants to stab you." I went towards him, and he ran away. She said, "Come on, Brian,

let's get out of here." She walked with me towards the exit. I was bleeding heavily now. A

police car pulled up, and I jumped in, asking the officer to take me to the hospital because I was stabbed and needed stitches. The policeman just drove around the block and came back to the city hall. He jumped out and said, "You come with me into the hall." I did not enter

Chapter 4

the hall; instead, I just stood outside. I heard someone say, "Brian." I looked around and saw it was a friend of mine. He said, "Come on, Brian, let me take you to the hospital."

I jumped into his car, and he sped off with a worried look on his face. Suddenly, I saw blue lights beside us—it was the police. My friend slowed down and explained that I had been stabbed and he was rushing me to the hospital. The cops drove in front of us and told us to follow them. When we arrived at the hospital, a policeman got a wheelchair and pushed me straight to emergency. My wounds were all stitched up. I had four stab wounds: one in my hand, two on my shoulder, and one in my back near my spine. Wounded, I called a taxi from a call box to take me home.

When I arrived at home, everyone was standing in the lane, talking and looking worried. They had probably all heard what had happened to me. I looked in the garage and saw that my car was there. A friend of mine had driven it home because I needed to go to the hospital. The next morning, a gang of guys from the district, who knew me, came to see me. They were quite a notorious gang and had heard what had happened to me. Revenge was all they wanted. I let them know I was badly wounded and all stitched up. The plan was to have a drink, then go and fight, which would cause unnecessary bleeding to my wounds. I didn't like the idea of gangsters coming to visit me at my home, so I got out of bed and walked them out of the house. They left, saying, "Tell us when you are feeling alright."

In the evening, I got a call from another district from my cousin, who said, "The guys that stabbed you at the city hall are sitting in a house nearby." He suggested that if my gang joined forces with his, we could surround the house and get them. Fortunately, a job came up in Sasol, a large industrial city in the far north of the Orange Free State, where fuel was made from coal. Sasol was five hours and forty-three minutes from Durban. I travelled there with three other men in my Chevy. We took a shortcut through Soweto.

Whilst driving through the township, I noticed lights flashing in my rearview mirror and saw a 4x4 behind me. I realised it was the police.

SET FREE

I tried pulling over but couldn't because of a curb. They continued to flash their lights at me to stop. Finally, I was able to stop, and they overtook me and stopped in front of my car. The Afrikaans policeman jumped out with guns, pointed at us, and ordered us to get out of the car immediately. They aggressively told us to put our hands on the roof of the car and started to search us. They asked whose car it was, and I told them it was mine. They ordered me to open the boot and started rummaging through our suitcases, throwing and mixing up our clothing. Roughly, they asked where we were going. I explained that we were going to work and that we lived at the campsite on the job, going home to our families every fortnight. The policeman indicated for me to close the boot and continue on our way.

Chapter 5
More Drama

My friend and I were on our way home from Greenwood Park. Driving down the road, I saw two guys hitchhiking. I decided to give them a lift. All of a sudden, a police van (ute) pulled up beside my car with two Afrikaans cops. One cop asked me why I had stopped on the side of the road. I looked at him and said, "I decided to give these two guys a lift." In the apartheid era, being a non-white meant one stood no chance. One was always looked at suspiciously, bossed around, and spoken to aggressively. This was their way of expressing their authority over non-whites. They could do whatever they pleased. They were in control. The cop looked at me and said, "Follow me to the police station."

The two guys had jumped in my car. They were from the area and sat in the back while my friend was in the passenger seat. As we drove off, following the cop van, they turned left. The cop in the passenger seat looked at me and indicated that he was watching me. These policemen packed guns and were trigger-happy; they wanted to shoot.

Indicating that I was going to turn to follow them, one of the guys in the back said, "Don't turn, I will direct you where you need to go." I accelerated and sped off, relying on the guy to direct me away from the cops. This was a main road, and as we continued driving, there was a road turning off to the right. The guy in the back said, "Turn here." I found myself driving up a hill. When I almost reached the crest of the hill, he told me to turn into a property. Turning quickly into the property, I drove behind a hedge and switched the car and lights off. I saw

SET FREE

the police van, blue lights flashing, continuing to chase us. The police van sped past us. Phew! They lost us. Taking a back route, I drove in the opposite direction. This was unnecessary, but it was the reality of the times we were living in. As a non-white, one could expect anything from the oppressor.

Working on the gold mines near Klerksdorp, my friends and I decided to go home for a few days and then return to work. The road trip to Durban was seven and a half hours. There were four of us in the car, including myself. We travelled three hours before we reached a little town called Bethlehem in South Africa, where our car broke down. This was an Afrikaans town where the people only spoke Afrikaans. My friend and I decided to hike to the town, leaving the other two guys to keep an eye on the car. We were trying to get help, probably a breakdown service, to get the car fixed.

It got dark, and it was late, so we decided to stay overnight in the town. The other two guys would have to sleep overnight in the broken-down car. Early the next morning, we woke up, washed up, and looked for a phone booth where we could make a call to ring for a breakdown service. To make this call, we needed loose change, as the phone booth only took coins.

This was our fortnight pay week. Our pay envelopes, stating how much we had earned and with our names was all printed on our payslips, contained cash. We saw a petrol station and walked towards it. Seeing the petrol attendant, we approached him and asked if he could please give us some change to make a call. He assumed we wanted to rob him. Robbery was quite common in these little towns. He started to get aggressive, speaking very angrily with us, chasing us away from the premises. My friend started to shape up for him, wanting to fight with him. This was unnecessary; all we were asking for was change, and now we were facing this attitude.

I turned around and saw another guy with a knife in his hand approaching us, trying to defend the petrol attendant. The guy with the knife was making his way towards my friend and had to come in my direction. He was fast approaching. When I was a little boy, I had learned

Chapter 5

a few karate stunts. I knew a few movements and had learned how to scream when attacking an opponent. Shaping up like a karate expert and making noises—*haaaaa!*—with determination, I walked towards him. The guy with the knife slowed down as he saw I was challenging him. My friend left the petrol attendant and came to assist me. The guy with the knife ran away as fast as he could.

Walking a distance away from all the drama, we sat on a wall next to a phone booth. It was still very early in the morning, so we decided to just wait until the shops opened to get some change. My friend and I were in a deep conversation when I looked up and saw a police truck with a detaining canopy. It was two Afrikaner police in a truck with the petrol attendant. The petrol attendant pointed to us and told the policemen that we were the two men who wanted to rob him.

The policemen jumped out of the van and walked over to us. We tried explaining ourselves, but their words to us in Afrikaans were, "We will talk at the police station." They put the two of us in the back of the police truck and drove to the station. A change of shift was happening at the police station, so there were policemen all over. I was English-speaking but knew Afrikaans, and so did my friend, so we could understand when we were spoken to. The station commander asked the policemen what we had done. The policemen told the station commander that the petrol attendant said we wanted to rob him. Taking out our payslips, we showed the station commander who we were and explained that all we wanted was to make a call for a breakdown.

The station commander took our payslips, looked at them, and said, "There is no way these men wanted to rob the petrol attendant. Look at the money these men earn."

The commander looked at us and asked, "What is it you need? What is the problem?" We explained that our car had broken down and we needed a tow truck to take our vehicle back to Klerksdorp. He agreed, called the tow truck, and told us to wait. The tow truck arrived, took us to the car, and towed it away. The four of us took a taxi back to Klerksdorp. Unfortunately, we didn't end up going home to Durban because the gearbox in the car had given out.

SET FREE

On the weekend, my friend and I were invited to a twenty-first birthday party. At the party, there were a few guys from Klerksdorp that we had worked with. Jealousy had developed toward us Durban guys because we weren't locals. We stood at the gate of the house, armed with daggers and knives. This was a boarding house for workers, including some Durban guys. The story was that guys from our district had sold drugs to the locals, who then didn't want to pay. These non-payers were part of a notorious gang from Johannesburg.

We entered the house, and a fight broke out. One of the Durban guys stabbed someone with a dagger. Another guy with a bald head was dancing with a girl. I approached him, and the girl screamed. I took my knife and scratched it on his head. He grabbed his gun and fired three shots into the air. We took cover and started running toward the gate. Everyone scattered in different directions.

I ran into a massive field with tall grass. I lay down in the grass, the moon shining bright, my heart beating fast. In the distance, police sirens blared, and commotion was heard nearby. I lay still, catching my breath. After a while, the sirens stopped, and it became quiet. I stood up slowly, looking around, and began to walk swiftly toward my uncle's house. As I got closer, I heard someone softly call my name, "Brian, come into the house." Feeling the need to protect myself, I held onto the dagger in my hand, just in case.

We found out that our transport to go back home had been sabotaged; all the wheels on the car were slashed and needed to be fixed. We couldn't stay here any longer. The next morning, we packed our bags and made our way home. No job and back home.

Chapter 6
Sharon

This way of life started to exhaust me, always on the run, dealing with trouble and violence. I finally realised I needed to settle down. I pondered going to Cape Town, thinking I might find a girl there. At the same time, I preferred to settle with someone in my own city, Durban. Less than 30 metres away, the government had built a block of apartments housing families. I was completely unaware that the girl I would marry lived there.

My best friend, Gilo, was my immediate neighbour; we were just a fence apart. I often went over to his house. He was married with a wife and baby, and I would always help with transport if they needed to go anywhere. On Boxing Day in December 1978, he asked if I could help load their luggage into my car. They were visiting his wife's family in Greenwood Park, a half-hour to forty-minute drive. I walked into the room to grab the luggage, not realising there were people inside. Looking up, I saw a beautiful girl sitting with my friend's wife and her relative.

They were laughing and chatting, and feeling a little nervous, I walked out with the luggage, making my way to the car. I opened the boot to pack the luggage. Turning around, I saw that the girl and her friend had come out of the house and were now sitting on the bumper of an old car parked in the front yard. I looked up and straight into her big, brown, smiley eyes. We both engaged, staring at each other. In that moment, something happened to me. I melted even more

SET FREE

when she continued to smile. Her stare was intense and indescribable. Nervously, I shoved the luggage into the boot.

Later, I asked my friend's wife about the girl—who she was, where she was from, where she lived. My friend's wife couldn't tell me much; she was just a friend of her relative.

One day, while driving on Austerville Drive, I saw a girl in a Wentworth High School uniform walking ahead on the same side of the road. I slowed my car down, driving slowly alongside her. She looked at me, and those familiar smiley brown eyes looked back. It was the same girl I had seen at my friend's house. I greeted her gently, but she did not answer; instead, she walked faster. I couldn't continue driving slowly, and she quickly disappeared into a lane ahead. I felt disappointed; I was attracted to this girl.

Another time, near my home, I saw her again. She seemed to be heading somewhere. I tried slowing the car down and talking to her, but she didn't respond. Suddenly, she disappeared into another lane. I wanted to stop and jump out of the car, but I thought better of it and continued driving home.

Coming back from Klerksdorp, reflecting on my life, with no job, I felt the need to settle down. I drove my Chevy to the top of the lane where I lived, something I didn't usually do; I would normally just walk up the lane. I parked my car facing the shopping centre, jumped out, and sat on the bonnet. The top of the lane was a meeting point where the guys would hang out. I saw this as an opportunity to catch up with them; it had been almost a month since I had seen my friends.

Looking across the field, I saw two girls walking toward the shopping centre. One of them looked very familiar—it looked like the girl with the big brown smiley eyes. I could feel my heart beating faster. I felt I had to meet this girl. The boy living next to me passed by in his school uniform, and I started talking to him. As we chatted, I kept an eye on the two girls. When they returned from the shopping centre, I asked my neighbour, who was in the same school, "Do you know this girl?" pointing to the one in the school uniform. He said, "Yes, I know her, Brian. She is a very nice person." I asked, "Could you introduce me to her?"

Chapter 6

He excitedly agreed. The other girl had already made her way home, leaving the girl I so desperately wanted to meet walking alone.

The lanes ran parallel to each to other with a row of houses in between. I drove my car down the lane to my house. My neighbour met up with this girl in another lane. When both lanes ended this is where all the apartments (flats) had been built. She was on her way home. My neighbour approached her and had mentioned I wanted to talk to her. I jumped out my car and made my way toward them. Feeling nervous, I thought she would walk away when she saw me coming, but she waited. As I got closer and finally stood right next to her, my neighbour introduced us to each other. Her smile and the glow in her brown eyes made my heart melt. The attraction was undeniable, just like the first time I had seen her on Boxing Day—a beautiful, radiant, elegant, and ladylike girl. I stood there feeling frozen, like a melting ice block.

Later, while dating her, she told me she had been astounded because I was the same guy she had felt attracted to. She had always tried to get away, more so to run from her feelings for me. Her name was Sharon.

Looking me straight in the eye, she asked, "Are you working?" I did not expect a question like that. Thinking quickly, I knew I had to answer wisely. It was a weekday after school (Friday), so what was I doing at home? I answered, "I am on leave." I was still uncertain about getting another job, so this seemed like the best answer, even though I wasn't being entirely honest. There was no way I was going to lose my heartthrob this time. I asked, "Would you take a drive with me? I would like to talk to you and get to know you." Sharon agreed but asked if she could go home first and then meet me in my lane. Feeling excited and nervous, I walked towards my car. I sat in the car and waited, anxious that she might not come back. Not long after, I looked up, my heart beating fast. There she was, walking towards the car, full of smiles.

I remember, before I jumped into my car, I ran into my house and asked, "Dad, do you have a five rand for me?" He grumbled but handed me the money. I was desperate, as I had no job. I already had a plan: I would drive Sharon to the beach. Driving my car, I couldn't

SET FREE

believe she was sitting next to me. I stopped at a shop while Sharon remained in the car. I bought two fresh cream doughnuts and two bottles of Fanta.

Arriving at the beach, I parked the car and we started talking. There were a few fishermen nearby, and Sharon asked, "What colour is the sea water?" Fortunately, I knew the answer. "The sea has no colour; the water is clear, and the colour it gets is from the sky," I said. I felt good about myself, feeling smart about my answer. We continued to talk. She told me she was a ballet dancer and a model, lived in the Austerville district, and had been living in my district for over a year without my knowing. She attended high school, with History and English as her favourite subjects. She was very involved in the school's modelling shows and concerts as a tap dancer.

There was something special about this girl—I really liked her. Coming for a drive with me made me feel good; she trusted me. Her beautiful, shy, and timid smile, the way she looked at me when she spoke, I knew she liked me too. I had never felt this way about a girl before. Being with her made my world stop for a second. We arranged another time to see each other, and as I drove her home, I mentioned how much I looked forward to seeing her again. She said, "Me too."

On Saturday morning, the next day, a friend of mine came to my house and said he had organised a job for me at the Amatikulu Tongaat Hulett Sugar refinery as a welder. I was happy knowing I would be working again. The job was a two-hour drive from home, and I would have to leave Sunday night to be there Monday morning. The Sugar Mill camp housed the workers on-site, meaning I would stay on the job and come home after three weeks. I sent a message to Sharon, letting her know I had to go to work and would be away for the next three weeks.

I was happy but sad—I really wanted to see Sharon again, and now I would have to wait three weeks. I started the job on Monday with my friend. That night, getting ready for bed, I told him, "I think I am in love; I met this beautiful girl, and I feel crazy about her." My friend assured me, "Brian, don't worry; she will wait for you." Later, I found out that during the three weeks I was away, Sharon would visit my

Chapter 6

friend's wife and spend time with their baby. This made her feel closer to me. She missed me and felt a sense of belonging being with the people I knew.

Three weeks passed, and I looked forward to seeing my girl again. We met and went out to the cinema, spending lots of time together, talking about us. Time didn't matter. I told Sharon I had been in a reformatory, and she listened attentively, so interested. I had never shared my stories with a girl before, and I felt so comfortable with her. She told me her uncle and cousin had been in a reformatory too. She mentioned their names, and I knew them; I remembered them.

Before moving into our district, Sharon, her mum, sister, and brother had lived with their grandmother in Austerville. This district had a lot of violence and gangsterism. The place we lived in was called Wentworth, but Austerville was worse, with the highest rate of violence. The crime stemmed from gang violence and drugs, leading to murder, robbery, and disreputable behaviour like gambling and unemployment. Sharon's cousins and uncle, who also lived with her grandmother, were part of a gang in the district.

Despite the violence, Sharon and her family were kept safe—no one dared to interfere with them. She was always told that her family would sort out anyone who interfered with her. They were very protective of her. Sharon was elegant, a model, always dressed in style with flowing long brown hair, sparkling brown eyes, and she carried herself like a princess. For me, she was not only beautiful on the outside but also had inner beauty—her character, mannerisms, morals, values, and the way she spoke. I loved her.

In Austerville, the boys knew me. One of my best friends from the reformatory lived there. Now Sharon had moved from Austerville and was living in my district. In my district, there was also a gang. Being a gangster or part of a gang gives you a bad reputation in the community. People start to have trust issues when your name is mentioned in conversation. You become part of the neighbourhood gossip, and often, half of the stories are not true. Among the community, you become branded, especially your name.

SET FREE

We continued to secretly date. Sharon was seventeen years old, still attending school and modelling classes on Saturdays. I would pick her up from modelling school on Saturdays, and we would spend the rest of the day together. She looked forward to being with me. I loved Sharon, and we enjoyed each other's company. She would listen to my stories, showing so much interest and compassion towards me. I felt comfortable with her and could express my thoughts and feelings without fear of judgment.

Our relationship felt like we had known each other forever. I wanted to spend the rest of my life with her. I decided to take her home to introduce her to my family. I had never taken a girl home to meet my family, but I loved her, and I wanted them to meet her. My mum was busy in the garden, and my dad and sister were in the house. My mum cleaned and dried her hands, then came inside to meet Sharon. I introduced her to my parents and sister. They shook her hand, smiling, and were happy to meet her.

Sharon, on the other hand, was afraid of how her mum would feel about the two of us. Sharon was still at school, and her mum was a single parent. She was strict and, like any mum, protective. At the time, I did not understand, but I do now, from a father's perspective. A relationship with a boy would be an uproar. Her mum felt she was still young and that there was still time for relationships.

We were in love and wanted to be with each other. Time was not a factor, although sometimes I would take her home early, but she would still want to be with me despite it getting late. I would be worried for her, and she would end up going home even later. My aunt once mentioned to Sharon, "What have you done to Brian? It was so strange finding him at home in his pyjamas; he has changed so much since meeting you." My friend's mother came to visit one day, and Sharon walked in the door all dressed up for a date. She told my friend's wife, "Brian has met a fine lady; she is so beautiful."

My ouma would be so excited to see Sharon that she would do a special dance, circling her and singing, "My Lady, My Lady." My eldest sister visited one day with her husband, who taught me welding. I was

Chapter 6

parked in my car, chatting with Sharon. I introduced her to my sister, and she said to Sharon, "Nice to meet you, Sharon; we have heard so much about you." My family really liked her, which made me feel good and confirmed how I felt about her. My sister, living at home at the time, really took a liking to her, and they got on so well whenever Sharon came to visit.

One day, we went out for the day and parked outside my parents' house. It was late at night, and I started to worry about the time, trying not to show her my concern. We were always so comfortable and relaxed around each other, talking, laughing, and sharing more stories. Suddenly, I heard a tap on my window and opened the door. It was Sharon's mother, and she was angry. Someone had told her we were sitting in the car. Sharon got out, and her mother walked up to her and slapped her across the face.

Now, as a dad and granddad, I totally understand her worry about her daughter being out so late. It broke my heart to see my girlfriend being slapped. Only love can fill the empty room in one's heart, and mine was overflowing. We continued to see each other and went out on dates. Our favourite spot at the time was along the Durban esplanade, where we could drive through and park our car. A waiter would come to our car, take our order, and in 10-15 minutes, bring a tray and place it on the open window. It was so romantic, just me and my girl. Strawberry milkshakes were our favourite, and they went perfectly with a hamburger. It was a popular place for couples.

One day, a guy from work and I talked about the races and decided to bet on a horse. I took Sharon to the racecourse, but embarrassingly, my horse came last—a real donkey, frothing at the mouth. I was just happy to be spending time with my girl. One day, I wanted to see Sharon, but her mother wouldn't let me. I had bought a box of chocolates for her and asked my friend to take it over to her house. He gladly offered to do this for me. This friend of mine was very comical. He knocked on the apartment door, and when Sharon answered, he loudly said, "Brian said I must give you this box of chocolates; he wants to let you know how much he loves you." Sharon's mother heard and

SET FREE

demanded the chocolates be sent right back. Later, I found out Sharon and her sister enjoyed them that night. Sharon told me it was such a beautiful chocolate box that she used it for her curlers.

For our first Christmas together, I bought Sharon a Delfin quartz gold watch from the jeweller's. The cost didn't matter; she was my everything, and I wanted to give her the best. She bought me expensive whisky, Ballantine's, a rare blend and an icon of luxury, all boxed and packaged.

I was always with my girl, hardly spending time with my friends. One Friday evening, I decided to spend time with some friends. We went to a dance at a hotel called "The Fountain" in a suburb called Sydenham, a twenty-five-minute drive from Wentworth. I parked my car, and we walked inside. We recognised a few guys I worked with who lived in the area. After having a few drinks and talking to the guys, one of them warned us, saying, "Brian, it's better you and the guys leave; the local Sydenham gang is coming here." We decided to leave. As I walked out with some friends, the others stayed behind to talk to the guys. By the time I reached my car and before I could open the door, a big gang arrived. We were outnumbered. They asked whose car it was, and I told them it was mine. They didn't believe me. One of them threw a broken asbestos gutter at me, hitting me above my right eye and cutting my eyebrow. Blood splattered all over my face.

The gang started moving towards us, intent on attacking. Amidst all the noise and commotion, my friends came out to see what was happening. My friend and I began to run down the road, away from the gang. As we were running, four guys broke from the crowd and started to chase us. We kept running, and I said to my friend, "We have to turn around, face them, and put fear in them." This gang knew where we came from. As we continued to run and the guys kept chasing us, my friend told me he was scared. I reassured him that we needed to keep running. I explained my plan: we would turn around and run towards them. My friend had no choice but to turn around with me and face them. We had no weapons and were caught off guard.

Chapter 6

Turning around and running towards them, I shouted loud and clear, "Let's just catch one, only one, and kill him." Hearing this, they turned around and ran for their lives. Seeing them run off, we turned around and hitched a lift with a van. A guy stopped to give us a ride.

Seeing my bloody face, he was scared and drove me straight to the hospital. At the hospital, I was cleaned up and received eight stitches on my eyebrow. Whilst getting stitched up, I felt angry, and all I could think of was revenge. We took a taxi home.

The next morning, Saturday, I gathered a few of the local gang friends from our district. We loaded my car with choppers, flick knives, slashers, and daggers. A big German shepherd dog, part of the gang, was loaded into the car too. First, we had a few drinks, prepping ourselves for the big gang fight. Everyone jumped into my car, and I drove off to Sydenham. I was furious. When we arrived, we noticed a few of them sitting in a park. I brought my car to a full stop. They saw us, recognised my car, and started to run. Relatives of one of our gang members lived nearby, so we went to their house. We caused a noisy scene, loudly asking, "Where are these gangsters?" and started looking for them in the road where they usually hung out.

A big dog jumped over the fence to attack us. Our gang let our dog out of the car to counterattack. Some of our gang members kicked the attacking dog, causing it to jump back over the fence, screaming. We realised the neighbours would soon call the police, so we drove back to our suburb. We weren't even with this gang, but we knew we had left an impression; it wasn't over yet.

I didn't see my girl that weekend. I was embarrassed about my eye and having been in a fight. On Monday, I was driving down the road and saw her walking up the road. I felt so bad driving past her but was too embarrassed. My heart throbbed, but I continued to drive. I really wanted to see her. While dating, Sharon would sometimes jump into my car and find knives under the seats. She got so used to finding knives that she would take them away from me. One day, I visited her with a gun under my jacket and showed it to her. Caring as always, she said, "Brian, you need to stop all of this." I knew she

SET FREE

loved me and showed concern despite my condition. She never saw or witnessed the other side of my life, although I did lose myself once when she mentioned one of the guys I knew had interfered with her. I approached him and slapped him across the face. He said he didn't know Sharon was my girlfriend and apologised. She was too dear to me, and I did not want to lose her. She was my girl, and I had to protect her.

Chapter 7
Arrested

Working on a construction site in Germiston, situated in the Transvaal near Johannesburg. Germiston was in the East Rand area of Johannesburg, the sixth largest city in South Africa. The drive from Durban to the Transvaal was over five hours. On-site, we were building a large molasses steel tank. My friend and I had come home for the weekend, and now we were returning to work. Before we started our journey, we purchased alcohol—a bottle of whisky called Southern Comfort and half a dozen of beers. This was going to be a good journey, just the two of us. Later, we got to find out the whisky was not a comfort at all.

We travelled in my friend's car, a Ford Fairlane 500 V8. This car had power, giving one a thrill when driving. We travelled through a little town called Cornelius, through the Orange Free State. Drinking and chatting was good until my friend started to feel drunk and tired. We had drunk quite a bit of whisky and beers. He said, "Brian, you take the wheel." By now, it was dark. Wanting to feel the car's power, I agreed to drive.

Driving through a rural area with no streetlights, the car sounded good. You could feel the power. I realised if I picked up speed, the journey would go faster. A big truck was traveling in front of me, and there was a barrier line, making it clear I could not overtake this truck. The truck was really going slow, and I started to feel annoyed and irritated. I would soon fall asleep if I continued driving at such a slow pace behind this truck. I decided to take a peek to see if the road was clear.

SET FREE

Noticing there was no oncoming traffic, I put my foot on the gas and overtook the truck. As I passed the truck, I saw a police car escorting it. Seeing this, I knew I would be in serious trouble for overtaking on a barrier line. I decided to make a clean getaway, putting my foot flat on the accelerator. After traveling a distance, I looked in the rearview mirror and noticed no policemen were chasing me. I looked at my friend, who was drunk, fast asleep, and unaware of what was happening.

Slowing down, thinking all was well, I saw a blue light flashing in my rearview mirror. The police car pulled up beside me, and the officer pointed his gun at me, indicating I needed to pull over. I pulled over, and the cop parked a distance in front of me. He walked towards me, still pointing his gun. I nudged my friend, shaking him, and telling him to wake up. "Wake up! There's the police. Wake up!" When the officer reached me, he said, "I almost shot you dead." This was during the apartheid era; if you were a non-white and spoke English, it meant more trouble. They wanted non-whites to speak Afrikaans. The Afrikaans police were ruthless and trigger-happy when it came to people of colour.

The cop asked me, "Who is the owner of the car?" I pointed to my friend, who had just woken up and was still drunk. "He is," I said. The policeman did not even check if my friend was drunk. He looked at my friend and said, "Take the wheel," then pointed to me and said, "You, jump into the van with me." My friend jumped into the driver's seat and followed the police car. I looked at my friend's face; he looked worried, and by now, he was sobered up.

Noticing a German Shepherd in a cage next to my seat, I decided there was no way I was going to sit next to the dog. I jumped into the front of the van. The police officer looked at me and said, "Get into the back seat." I found myself sitting in the back seat, staring at the dog. The policeman drove off, and my friend followed. We stopped at a police station in Cornelius, but it was closed, and no one was around. There was a house next door, and the police officer jumped out of the car and started throwing stones at the roof. I assumed another police officer lived there, and he needed to get up to open the station. After a

Chapter 7

while, a private vehicle drove by, and a police officer in civilian clothes opened the police station.

My friend and I stood in the charge office while the two policemen walked to the back and started having a discussion. I spoke loudly, wanting them to hear me, "I may need a lawyer." One of the police officers heard me and said, "What did you say?" He violently grabbed me by the back of my shirt, took me outside, and pushed me into a pitch-black cell. I could see nothing. Entering the cell, I knew I would need to protect myself. Speaking in Afrikaans in a threatening voice, I said, "Where is my blanket? Where do I sleep?" It worked, and soon I had a blanket in my hand. I tried sleeping, but I couldn't. Being in a strange place, I didn't even know who I was with in this cell.

The next morning, I was removed from the cell with other prisoners, put in a van, and taken to another police station. From there, we were taken to court in Freda. I was found guilty and given a speeding fine of one hundred rand or one hundred days in jail. Not having enough money on me at the time, I had to go to jail. A convicted guy approached me and said that once we were in jail, we should look out for each other in case anyone tried to interfere with us.

Entering the jail, there were two sections: a grilled yard with gates leading into a cell. We stood together when one of the inmates came up to us, saying, "Don't stand outside. You need to find a place to sleep. Come in." Entering the cell, I decided to go in first, but then backed off and let the other guy go first. I didn't know what to expect and feared an unexpected attack. It seemed a bit cowardly, but jail was all about survival.

Sitting on the floor on blankets, one of the inmates pointed to a Bible and asked me, "Do you know this book?" I looked at him and said, "No." Although I grew up in a Christian home—my family was Anglican—I never went to church. I told him I didn't know about the book and didn't understand the Bible. Deep down in my heart, I knew there was a GOD. Memories flooded my mind. I was ten years old when my mum took me to the priest because I was a naughty boy and wasn't listening. The priest gave me a long, hard talk, and I listened attentively.

SET FREE

The priest's last words to me were, "You don't love GOD." Those words affected me deeply, and I burst into tears. I was so emotional and thought, how could he say those words to me? I did love GOD. It was probably around 9 or 10 pm when I heard keys in the cell door, and the lights came on. Two Afrikaans policemen stood there with guns in their holsters. They started speaking Afrikaans to us and looked at one of the guys in the cell with us. I looked up, hoping I was going to be released, but instead, the policeman looked at me and said, "You come too." They took four of us out of the cell, locking the gate behind us, leaving other prisoners there.

They took us outside; it was very dark and seemed late into the night. One of the policemen told us to walk in front of them and make our way to the police van. This van had a cage at the back. As we walked to the van, one of the policemen said, "Run a little because I want to shoot someone dead tonight." We slowed down, walking closer to the policemen.

Arriving at the van, the policemen ordered one of the men with us to remove the guy lying at the back of the van, and another guy assisted. The policemen then opened the door of a building, which I realised was a mortuary. The guys carried the body into the mortuary and were instructed to leave it on the floor. The dead person had sneakers on his feet (takkies). Entering the building, I noticed stainless steel stretchers on shelves. The policeman looked at me and said, "You search his pockets." Hesitantly, I searched and took money out of his pockets. Handling a dead man made me feel so uncomfortable. The other prisoners were standing around watching. They were then ordered to put the body on a stainless stretcher back on the shelf.

Witnessing all this, I pretended I couldn't handle it, working with a dead person. The police told me to come and stand next to him. Whilst standing there, he asked, "How much money is there?" I put the money on the table, and the policemen counted it and documented it in a book.

The policemen then turned to me and asked, "Why are you here?" I said, "I was driving fast; I was speeding." He pointed to the dead man

Chapter 7

on the shelf and said, "You see what fast driving does?" I already figured it out; there was no way this was due to fast driving. The dead man's pants were damp; he could have been running from the police. These policemen thought nothing of shooting someone. The prisoners seemed suspicious; the dead man was shot, which was why he was brought so late to the mortuary. Before walking out of the mortuary, one of the policemen pointed to the shelves and said, "Can you see there is enough space here for more bodies? So when you leave the building, just run." He was trying to convey that if we ran, he would shoot us dead. We were all taken back to the cell. Later that night, I heard footsteps in our cell; one of the prisoners was pacing and couldn't sleep after seeing the dead body. It affected him deeply. I really needed to get out of there soon.

The next morning, we were woken up and six of us were loaded like baggage into a small ute with a cage, all squashed up. An African policeman and a white policeman were arguing. The African policeman was trying to tell the white policeman that we were going to travel quite a distance and the tire needed changing. The white policeman adamantly refused to listen. They drove from Freda police station to Standerton Prison. The distance from Cornelius to Freda was 43.2km, which is a 26-minute drive, and from Freda to Standerton, it was 63.9km, a 46-minute drive, all bundled up in the back of a caged ute. In three days, I had been to three prisons. Standerton Prison housed all the hardened prisoners who were serving sentences for murder, robbery, and other serious crimes, including those pulling five to eight years and life sentences. Here I was, with a minor offence, placed among hardened criminals. I realised that this is how some people with no intentions of becoming criminals end up hardened through minor offences.

Leaving Freda and heading to Standerton to serve our time, all bundled in the van, became very scary. The white Afrikaans policeman was driving the van very recklessly. The back tire flew off, and he lost control. Fortunately, we went over an embankment that was not too steep, so the van did not roll. The policeman came to the back of the van, opened it, and reached for his gun, saying, "Get out,

SET FREE

and if any of you run, you will be shot." There was no spare wheel to change the tire. Fortunately, another similar ute drove by, and the driver stopped and lent his spare tire to the policeman. They managed to complete the journey to Standerton Prison. Arriving at the prison, I couldn't wait to get out. Six of us jam-packed in a closed ute was very uncomfortable.

I was taken to the warden. He took me to a room and instructed me to take off my clothes and get dressed in a prison outfit: a hat, trousers, shirt, brown shoes that were too big for me, and socks so long I had to fold them under my feet. The warden said, "You will need to shave, and if nobody comes for you by 3 pm today, you will have to shave your hair off too."

Standing in the courtyard, I felt lost, thinking to myself what I had gotten into. I was working, earning good money, had met the girl of my dreams, and here I was. I stood on the one side of the courtyard, lots of other prisoners standing on the other side. I chose not to stand amongst them; I did not know what crimes they had committed. Then I heard, "Brian." Someone called my name or was I imagining. How could someone know me here, so far away from home? Seeing someone walk towards me, this person said, "Brian, don't you remember me?" I said, "Yes, I do." I could not remember his name, but I did remember he was part of my cousin's gang. He said, "My name is Chillies." Still in the apartheid era at the time, he said, "Brian, don't worry, I work in the kitchen. I will give you what the white prisoners eat." The white prisoners ate better than the non-white prisoners. Lunch would be served at 11 am, and he told me where I needed to be at lunchtime.

All the prisoners made their way to the dining hall. The men would sit in groups of three, in rows on their haunches. Three prisoners at a time would enter the dining hall and be seated at the table. When everyone was seated, the food was served to us in steel bowls. Chillies came to my table, bringing me the food meant for the white prisoners and taking my non-white food away. The other prisoners noticed this and started grumbling; they were not happy. Chillies loudly said,

Chapter 7

"Brian, don't worry about them, just eat your food." I couldn't see the difference—all the food looked the same to me. I ate some of the food, having little appetite. After lunch, all the prisoners left the dining hall and made their way back to the courtyard. I was standing, looking around. Chillies came to me and said, "Brian, you must go and be with the other guys, don't worry." He added, "Come, let me take you around and show you the cells." The cells were large, and each prisoner was given two blankets: one to roll up for a pillow and one to sleep on.

Chillies advised, "Brian, if you're going to stay tonight, wait until everyone goes to their bed. When you see an empty bed, head for it; otherwise, if it's someone's bed, it will cause trouble." We talked, and Chillies gave me a comic to read. Three o'clock was dinner time, and I remembered that if nobody came to pick me up by this time, I would have to shave my head. Walking to the dining room for dinner, we followed the same procedure: sitting in rows of three on our haunches, waiting. Chillies approached me, saying, "Brian, don't worry about queuing for dinner, your supervisor is here to take you out." I breathed a sigh of relief—no shaving my head. Chillies took me to the warden, who said, "You are going out. There is your bag; change into your clothes and put your prison clothes into the bag." I changed into my clothes, and the warden took me to the Station Commander who was in charge. Walking to the Station Commander, I looked outside towards the big gates and saw my supervisor standing there, smiling.

The Station Commander asked me, "So, how was it in the prison?" I wanted to get out of there, so I looked at him and said, "Everything was okay." I was escorted to the gate and they let me through. My supervisor paid the one-hundred-rand speeding fine. I couldn't believe I had gone through all of this for a speeding fine—two jails and one prison in three days. Driving back to the job with my supervisor, he mentioned how he went to the first prison only to find I had already left for the second prison. He had to return to the site and try again the next day, but the same thing happened—I had moved to the third prison. On the third day, he managed to find me at Standerton Prison. I was so happy

SET FREE

to be away from all of this and couldn't wait to be back home. This experience gave me an insight into the jail and prison world. When the Station Commander asked how my time in jail was, I could have spoken up about how I felt, but I chose not to. I just wanted to get out of that place.

Chapter 8
Getting Married

I had missed my girl; I was so happy to see her again. I did not give her the full details of my story or exactly what had happened to me. She did notice my moustache was shaved off. At the right time, I was going to tell her my full story. I felt I needed a change, so I decided to trade in my Chev Constantia and buy another car. I thought this would be the best—a new start. I bought a Chevrolet 4100, a silver-grey sedan with a white hard top. Chevrolet was my kind of car. Buying another car, I thought it would make a difference.

I continued to date Sharon secretly; her mum did not know. When her mum did find out, she was not happy, especially hearing false rumours about me. Jealousy thrived in our community. Family members and my own friends spoke about me, spreading untrue things. Sharon broke off our relationship; she felt there were just too many problems. This broke my heart in two. I told her, "I will be your puppet; you just pull the strings."

Breaking off our relationship did not last long. Sharon walked away and was back in five minutes. Her words to me were, "Brian, I thought about it. I cannot do this." We loved each other, and ending our relationship was not going to work.

I asked Sharon to marry me, to be my wife, the mother of my children. She was excited. Her mum, at the time, felt she was still young and needed more time. My reputation in the community did not make things easier. My parents were pressuring me, and everything became too much. I left home and went to board at a friend's house. There were lots of shortcomings, trials, and storms that came our way. It was not easy for the two of us; we wanted to be together, but it seemed so impossible. We both pushed through our trials, standing strong together. It took a lot of perseverance and time until things changed.

On November 29, 1980, we had a small twilight wedding at the Catholic church. My family and Sharon's family attended the wedding. I could not believe I was finally getting married to the girl I loved. Sharon, too, was beside herself with happiness. I remember preparing my car with white ribbon. The plan was for my sister to pick up Sharon and her bridesmaid from the apartment and drive them to the church. My brother was my best man. We borrowed Sharon's bridesmaid's boyfriend's car. He did not attend the wedding but agreed we could use his car.

We waited in the church as people started to arrive. The organ began to play, and I turned around to see my beautiful bride standing there, smiling and looking radiant. Sharon walked towards me, teary-eyed with a bouquet in her hand. Tears of happiness and joy filled the moment. Finally, our day had come. I will always remember the hymn sung at our wedding, "There shall be showers of blessing."

Earlier in the day, it had poured with rain, but by the time of our twilight wedding, the weather was perfect. The rain had stopped, and the stars were shining brightly in the sky. Our families congratulated us with smiles on their faces. After the wedding ceremony, I realised that the car we had borrowed to get to the church was no longer there. The bridesmaid's boyfriend had come during the ceremony and driven the car away. I managed to sort things out with my family to get transport for my brother, and I joined Sharon in my own car.

We gathered with our families at my parents' house for dinner and celebrations. All the troubles and problems seemed to vanish, and it was heartwarming to see our families together in harmony. It made our day.

My cousin drove Sharon and me to our new home in Clare Estate. Six months before the wedding, I had purchased furniture and homeware and found a rented place. This home was locked and paid for until

Chapter 8

we were married and able to move in. I had been patiently paying rent for this home, waiting for everything to work out for us.

We were so happy to be with each other; it felt like a dream come true for me. Waking up next to her was unbelievable. Sharon often mentioned dreaming of school and home, and she would say, "I am so happy to spend the rest of my life with you." We lived in a suburb far away from our families. After all we had been through, we wanted to be alone together. We did not visit family and instead stayed in our little nest.

Months later, Sharon's mother visited with a friend to see how she was doing. Her mother was quite surprised to see how I had set up our home for the two of us. I think she felt a sense of relief, especially after all the rumours and stories about me. I was happy, finally settled with a marriage, a car, and a rented home. My place of work was in Jacobs, a suburb near Wentworth, and I would travel quite a distance to work every day. My brother-in-law worked at the same company. Fridays were payday, and on Friday nights, Sharon and I would go grocery shopping. It was so affordable with just the two of us, and we always had petrol in the tank.

We had a beautiful, adorable baby girl by then, and she just completed our lives. She was Daddy's girl. Sharon always went to church on Sundays, and we would go together, visiting either the Anglican church or the Catholic cathedral in the city. Church was not something I was particularly interested in, but I went with Sharon because we were now a family.

We lived in a suburb called Clare Estate on Spencer Road. I no longer felt the desire to see my friends; my interest had waned. I felt so settled in my life. My wife, baby, and my own family were my priority. All we wanted was to make each other happy. Sharon took care of the baby and the home, while I continued to work and provide for my family, trying to keep up the pace. I would wake up early, doing physical training to stay fit and keep my family safe.

On Saturday mornings, we would go to Mitchells Park or take a boat ride along the harbour. Often, we would go to the beach, frolicking in the water with our little one. She loved the beach. On the way home, we would pass the butcher and buy tenderised steak. Sharon would cook a tomato chutney with green chilies and fry the steak, our Saturday favourite for lunch.

In the early evening, we would listen to programs on the radio. "Squad Cars" and "Consider Your Verdict" were my favourites. Surprisingly, television never interested us; we didn't have one. We preferred listening to the radio. Sharon's favourites were "Father, Dear Father," "Playhouse," and "High Adventure."

Milo and biscuits were always on the agenda later in the evening. We were so happy and really took time out for ourselves. At work, my brother-in-law, who was a preacher at the time, would talk to me about stories in the Bible. I was still set in my ways and not particularly interested in the things of GOD. Although I listened to him, the stories about Moses and the children of Israel did not resonate with me. He told me how the Israelites were afraid for GOD to talk to them and preferred that Moses speak on His behalf.

I would buy the newspaper on my way home and read it when I got there. Sharon did not like the idea of me reading the newspaper after work; she felt it took away from our time together. One day, as I was reading the paper, she came towards me and stood in front of it, indicating that she wanted my attention. Realising her feelings, I bought tickets to take her out to a show called the "Coon Carnival" at the Alhambra Theatre, wanting to spend more time with her. I organised for my sister to babysit our daughter, as the show was in the evening. My sister, who lived with my parents and adored our baby girl, was excited to have her over. We dressed up for the show and drove to my parents' house.

Chapter 9
Tent Campaign (1981)

In 1981, Wentworth had become rife with crime. Fortunately, many local churches were fighting to end the cycle of violence, which mostly stemmed from gang activity, drugs, or locals defending their area from unscrupulous outsiders. Churches held Tent Campaigns on a field near residential areas. One evening, while a tent campaign was being held, my wife and I left our baby at my parents' home and prepared to go to the show. When we arrived, my wife chatted with my sister in the kitchen while I sat down in the lounge to watch television. I heard some singing coming from the tent campaign. Although I had heard this type of singing before and never felt drawn to it, this time was different.

As I sat and listened to the music, I felt a tug in my heart to walk to the tent. I told my wife that I was leaving the car and just taking a walk to the top of the road, assuring her I would be back soon. When I arrived at the tent, I stood at one of the entrances. One of the believers came out to invite me in, but I told him I was on my way somewhere and couldn't stay. However, as I continued to stand there, they sang a song with the words, "There's going to be a meeting in the air, GOD's own son will be the leading one." I felt a heavy conviction and knew I needed to make my peace with GOD. It felt almost impossible to walk away.

I must have been there for a while because soon my wife and sister came looking for me. My wife said, "Brian, we need to go. It's getting late for the show." I asked if we could wait a little while, but eventually, we had to leave. We walked down to the car, kissed and hugged our baby goodbye, and drove off to the show. Sitting next to my wife, the show seemed dull. Even though there was lighting on the stage, the whole auditorium felt dark. I couldn't understand why, but I had lost all interest in being there.

Feeling uncomfortable, I felt the urge to leave. I had brought my wife to the show and felt bad about suggesting we go, as she was enjoying it and laughing. I sat there with no enthusiasm, finding the show boring and eagerly waiting for it to end. My wife was unaware of the strong conviction I was feeling to repent and make my peace with the LORD JESUS CHRIST. I didn't know much about being born again or serving GOD as people said. After the show, we drove home; our baby girl would be spending the night with my sister at my parents' house.

Usually, after a show or movie, we would chat about it, but this night was different. We entered the house, and I stood by my wardrobe door, wanting to change out of my clothes. I stood there for a while, staring into the wardrobe, thinking about how I was going to let my wife know what I was going through. Suddenly, she asked me, "Brian, how was the show?" She asked because she noticed I was quiet, which was not normal. Struggling to answer her, I knew my mind wasn't on the show. Turning around and looking at my wife, I said, "Sharon, I need to make my peace with GOD." I knew it sounded confusing to her. This was not the answer she expected. Instead of answering her question, I mentioned my need to make peace with GOD. She looked at me and said, "You took me out of the Catholic church. I started going to your church, the Anglican church."

I only attended the Anglican church as a little boy, and as I got older, church didn't matter to me. Marrying Sharon, she made sure we would go to church on Sundays. On the Sundays we attended the Catholic church in the city, I would sit behind the cathedral pillars with Sharon, avoiding eye contact with the priest. When it came to saved or born-again churches, I knew nothing about them. My wife, however, knew about them and said, "Now I must go to a saved church."

Chapter 9

Sharon's grandmother and uncle were born again, so she was familiar with the background. Mentioning that I wanted to make peace with GOD, I thought my wife would be happy, but she knew what lay ahead—lots of changes she wasn't ready for. Thanking GOD for a good wife, she didn't commit herself but was flexible and went along with me. There was a charismatic movement in the Anglican Church, defined as Christians who share with Pentecostals an emphasis on the gifts of the Spirit but who remain part of the mainline church. I joined this movement.

There were lots of other young married couples like Sharon and me. We would meet sincerely and have cottage meetings in people's homes. Some days during the week, it would be announced that a charismatic meeting would be happening in the basement of the church building. One night, Sharon and I attended the meeting.

People were being called up for prayer. I boldly walked to the front and knelt down. The priest asked what my request was, and I told him I wanted to serve the Lord and surrender my life to Jesus Christ. Some people in the meeting clapped and praised the Lord, knowing the life I had been living and witnessing GOD's work in changing me.

My job came to an end, and I needed work. My brother-in-law told me they were hiring in the Bayhead area, where oil rigs were being built. I needed this job. This was my first experience seeing GOD come through for me, opening a door of employment. Standing at the gate, I didn't know that six welders were going to be hired that morning. A recruiting supervisor came to the gate calling out, "Where are the six welders we are hiring this morning?"

Standing next to me was one of the welders to be hired, and he knew me. He said, "Brian, the sixth welder is not here today. He's not coming. You can fill his place." This needed to be confirmed with the supervisor, who had to make the final decision on who would replace the missing welder. The welder next to me raised his hand, indicating to the supervisor that I could take the place. Keeping me in suspense, the supervisor stood thinking for a while. He looked at me and said, "Okay,

SET FREE

you just get one chance with your weld test." Thank you, Lord, I was so happy. The six of us walked through the gate.

During my test, a former policeman who was now a welding supervisor recognised me. He spoke to the guy administering the welding test and said that when I was done, I could come and work in his section. The test administrator replied with an attitude, "I will send Brian where I want to." Later, the welding supervisor returned, and the test administrator looked at me and said, "You can go with him."

As I walked away to work in the supervisor's section, I felt the need to let him know upfront that I was now born again and living a completely different life. He knew the old Brian. His response was, "Oh, so good, Brian. Good to hear." He said he would introduce me to a brother serving the Lord in his section.

Arriving at the section where I was to work, the welding supervisor introduced me to a brother in the Lord named Colin. Getting to know Colin was a blessing. He attended the Baptist church, and looking back, I realised GOD had sent Colin my way. He was a real spiritual encouragement, telling me about church meetings during lunch breaks and times of fasting and praying on certain days.

On weekends, I looked forward to going to the Christian book room in the city. They sold Christian books and music, and Sharon and I would spend hours there, looking at all the spiritual literature. It was so interesting, like food for my soul. We would always go home with books to read.

Mixing with different believers from various denominations, I started to see things in the Anglican church that were not according to scripture. Feeling hindered, I approached the priest concerning baptism. There was no infant baptism in the Bible. Why did we sprinkle babies with water?

Scripturally, GOD requires us to be baptised in the name of the Lord Jesus Christ, being immersed in water to identify with His death, burial, and resurrection. Romans Chapter 6, verses 3 and 4 state: "Know ye not that so many of us as were baptised into Jesus Christ were baptised into his death? Therefore, we are buried with him by baptism into

Chapter 9

death: that like as Christ was raised up from the dead by the glory of the Father, even so we also should walk in newness of life." The priest couldn't give me a proper answer. He tried explaining, but it was not according to scripture. I knew I had to leave. I was worried about my wife and started to pray for her; she too needed to surrender her life to Christ. Her mother remarked that she would end up just like me and go to the saved church. Sharon answered her mother, saying, "I will never change." Colin and I fasted three times a week, trusting GOD for the meetings we would have on the job, winning souls for the Lord.

Colin invited me to his church to hear a visiting preacher. I took my wife and child along. Another time, we watched the movie, *Burning Hell*, at his church. The movie depicted the fate of non-Christians, showing eternal torment in hell. Colin asked me to bring blank cassettes to work so he could record gospel music for me to play in my car and at home. Listening to gospel music greatly encouraged me, and it felt like GOD placed Colin in my life at the right time. I needed someone older to draw spiritual inspiration and wisdom from. GOD bless my friend, Brother Colin. On the job, the Christian guys, including Colin and me, would sing gospel choruses. I realised GOD was really taking care of me after my conversion, placing me among believers where I could be spiritually uplifted and strengthened. I was so thankful to GOD for this. Some Fridays, on our payday, Colin would bring salvation tracks to work. There would be two queues formed at the payout windows.

Almost 200 men would form two lines for their pay. Colin would hand me some tracks, and starting from the front of each row, he would do one row while I did the other, ensuring each worker received a track. Once I reached the end of the queue, I would join the last guy and stand behind him for my pay. The oil rigs we worked on were jacked up on big wooden blocks, creating shade to sit underneath. One day, I was sitting under the rig reading a Christian book. Feeling thirsty, I went to the tap for a drink of water. When I finished, I looked up and saw my friend walking towards me. He had been my friend in reformatory and was a gangster in another area. Getting closer, he looked up into the sky and said, "Brian, we don't even thank the Lord for His creation."

SET FREE

I was surprised to hear him speak this way, especially knowing the life he came from. Feeling good and knowing I was born again, I could relate to him. We had a good conversation, talking about the Lord and glorifying Him.

Bringing back to my remembrance, the day we watched a movie together in reformatory, I noticed tears in his eyes and asked him what was wrong. He said he remembered telling me that nothing was wrong with him. A year later, he left reformatory for good. Another year passed, and here we were meeting at the tap on a job together. He said that the day we watched the movie, *The Cross and the Switchblade*, it brought tears to his eyes. He felt so moved and convicted while watching the movie that he felt he needed to make his peace with GOD. I felt so good talking to him; it was a great encouragement to see how GOD was working in people's lives. This friend of mine is a pastor today in Cape Town.

Chapter 10
Testimonies/Challenges

We started to have landlord issues relating to hot water usage. Sharon would wash our baby's nappies in hot water, which the landlord did not like. Then other minor issues began to arise. I decided to buy the newspaper and search for rented houses. The next day at work, during our 9 am morning break, I felt a strong, unexplainable presence. I turned around to Colin and said, "I feel my wife has given her life to Christ."

Arriving home after work, I walked into the house and looked towards the kitchen where my wife was. She stood there with a radiant smile on her face, her smile exhibiting joy and filling the room with warmth. Smiling back at her, I said, "You have given your heart to the Lord." She answered me, "Yes, how did you know?" I asked her what time it was when she made her decision. She answered, "9 a.m.," the exact time I had mentioned it to Colin. I felt such joy in my heart, knowing that from now on, we would serve the Lord together.

The two of us stood together, strengthening our marriage and making us stronger to face the challenges ahead. I praised GOD for my wife. Both of us, with one mind and one accord, had one goal in mind: to live for Jesus Christ. GOD made a way for us, and we found a house in the heart of Wentworth. We were closer to our families and the church. The place we lived in was not ideal, as the rooms were not connected to each other. To enter a room, we had to walk outdoors first.

We lived in this house until my parents offered for us to come and live with them. My mum was still working at Wentworth Hospital.

SET FREE

Working an evening shift, after work, I would go to the hospital to pick her up. Whilst waiting for her, I used the opportunity to visit the sick in the hospital, handing out salvation tracks to the patients in the ward. However, we could not continue living with my parents. As a family, we needed our own space and independence. I started house hunting again, looking for a rented place. Some of our friends in the Anglican church knew of a place and recommended it to us.

It was a very tiny place, just a bedroom, kitchen, toilet, and shower in a small room, with a very narrow passage at the entrance. The size didn't matter as long as we were together in our own space. We even had a place to park our car under a tree next to our little house. Baptism convicted me, and I wanted to do everything according to scripture. I left the Anglican church and went to a more scriptural and Pentecostal church. It was good to kneel down at night and pray with my wife before going to bed. We both started to look at life from a new perspective. Holiness, obedience, and serving GOD were all that mattered to us. We were sold out for Christ and happy. Sharon was two months pregnant with our second child when we both got baptised in a river in the name of the Lord Jesus Christ. For me, this was a profound spiritual experience. Water baptism symbolised Jesus Christ's death, burial, and resurrection, dying to the old self, and becoming a new creature in Christ Jesus.

We were happy in our rented home. I had a job, a car, and we were serving GOD. One day after work, I arrived home with the company driver. I got out of the car, limping and using crutches. My highly pregnant wife came to the doorway to see who was coming. When she saw me hopping out of the car on crutches and limping towards her, she was shocked and became emotional, sobbing continuously. I reached out to her, hugged her, and told her it was going to be alright; it was an accident at work. She couldn't contain herself and held me tight, still sobbing. Later, when we were settled, I explained to her about the accident at work.

I was working on an oil rig, on the mat footing of the rig, in a tank. The tank was very big with built sections. From the top of the tank,

Chapter 10

I had to enter a manhole and climb down a cat ladder to enter the tank. A section in this tank needed to be welded. To reach the job to weld, I had to stand on a scaffold. The supervisor at the time had come to the job with me to show me what I needed to do. Noticing there was only one scaffold plank, and it was warped, I mentioned this to him, but he insisted it was a small job and I needed to get it done.

I stood on the scaffold, positioned myself, and started welding. Suddenly, the scaffold plank flipped over, causing me to lose my balance and fall further into the tank. Moving my foot and concentrating on my welding likely caused the scaffold to move and flip. The bottom of the tank had angle irons, and my foot landed on one, causing it to twist and sprain. I was alone in the tank with no one to help me. I felt tremendous pain and a throb in my foot. I pulled myself up, holding on, and hopped towards the cat ladder, which would take me to the top of the tank. I looked up, placed my hands on the cat ladder, and pulled myself up. Every step was agony, and I prayed, "Lord, help me." My foot throbbed, but I finally reached the top of the manhole. I laid over the top, with only half of my body peeping out, trying to keep the wounded foot up. My other foot was on the ladder as I laid over the top of the tank. I was exhausted from the effort of trying to climb the cat ladder in excruciating pain. Some workers nearby rushed towards me, realising I was hurt.

The workers picked me up and carried me to the first aid station. The first aid attendant looked at my foot; it was swollen, dark blue, and throbbing continuously. I needed medical attention. They arranged for me to be transported to a medical centre. An x-ray was done, my foot was bandaged, and I was given a pair of crutches to use for walking. The company driver took me home.

Relating this story to my wife disturbed her; seeing me hurt was hard for her. For the next three weeks, I did not attend work. The company driver would pick me up and take me to the medical centre for physio sessions and then drop me back home. The company paid my wages every week, so I was still able to provide for my family. During those three weeks, my wife had to visit the hospital for her pregnancy

SET FREE

check-ups, and I took care of our toddler at home, hopping around on crutches. It was hard, but I managed. I would feed her, tidy her up, and try my best to comb her hair. My wife would return from the hospital, laughing at our toddler's hairdo.

On Sundays, despite my injury, I still attended church with my family. One of the brethren offered to drive my car to get us to church. The deacon always made sure I was comfortable, positioning my foot on a chair. I struggled, but GOD intervened and healed my injured foot, for which I am grateful.

Jobs became very scarce in the engineering, especially in the welding industry. Recession hit Durban, and many people were struggling to find work. Despite the tough times, I continued to serve GOD and trust Him to make a way for me. I remained strong for my family and looked to the Lord. Attending church services and fellowshipping with my brothers and sisters kept us going. Every day I would go out to look for work and come back with nothing. The cupboards were bare, with no food. With petrol almost empty in the car, we would visit my mum. Her words, "I was waiting for you two, I even cooked pumpkin for the baby," comforted us. Sharon's mum came to visit from Johannesburg one day, noticed our situation, and took Sharon to the supermarket, filling the trolley with groceries. We were so thankful, recognising how GOD was using even family members to meet our needs. It was tough, but I fasted and prayed, trusting GOD.

One day, after I had gone out to look for work, Sharon, now highly pregnant, was at home with our toddler, who was asleep in the bedroom. Sharon became hungry, but there was no food to eat. She fell to the kitchen floor and cried out, "Lord, I am so hungry right now." Being pregnant, she craved certain foods like sausages, putu, and chutney. As she wept on the floor, she heard her name being called. She got up, dried her eyes, and walked towards the door. The voice was familiar—it was the neighbour. The neighbour stood there with a plate covered with a dishcloth and said, "Here, take this; I cooked lunch for you." Sharon took the dish and walked into the house. When she removed the dishcloth, she saw sausages, putu, and chutney right before her

Chapter 10

eyes. Sharon sobbed, realising that GOD had provided for her in her moment of need. The GOD I served had made a way for my highly pregnant wife. Sharon was so excited to share this testimony with me. Even though I still had no job, I was excited that the Lord was with us.

On October 23, 1982, GOD blessed us with a second child, a beautiful baby girl. She had a mop of hair; I had never seen a baby with so much hair. She looked like a doll. I felt blessed and loved by GOD, who had given me a good wife and two beautiful daughters.

Four months had passed, and I still had no job. Our family had grown, and we needed a bigger place. We had no hot water or kitchen sink. Sharon's grandmother gave her a huge pot to boil water on the stove for baths. To wash the dishes, my wife would put the baby on her back, carry a basin full of dishes and dishwashing liquid, and walk seven metres with our toddler to the sink. She would wash up there and repeat the process for our laundry, carrying two buckets, a washing board, washing powder, and sunlight soap. While she worked, our toddler played in the yard. My wife would hang our washing under the tree on a clothesline.

This routine continued for a few months until the landlord installed a kitchen sink at the entrance of our home, making it easier for my wife to wash the dishes. Despite these challenges, we were happy. It did not interfere with our relationship. We loved each other and trusted GOD to help us stay strong for Him and each other. We lived simply, but when you are in Christ, He is all that matters.

Time moved on, and I still could not find work. I tried not to let it get to me, but the human side started to take over, and it slowly began to bother me. My family depended on me, and I depended on GOD for work. I needed to provide for them. Every month, I received unemployment benefits for the first three months, then I would have to reapply.

When I was newly married, I had purchased a wooden lathe for a bargain, thinking of the carpentry I had learned in reformatory and looking forward to using it in the future. I had put some money aside from my unemployment benefit and invested in a jigsaw and a drill. A plan came to me. With the little bit of carpentry I knew, I decided to put it into

SET FREE

practice. I purchased some pine wood and started making wooden side tables and spice racks with a paper towel holder.

My sister and her husband allowed me to use their garage to cut the wood. Early in the morning, my wife, toddler, baby, and I would go there. My wife stood by my side, giving me a hand with the baby on her back. She would sandpaper and varnish the spice racks. I worked hard, and it helped us bring in a few rands to buy food, pay rent, and put petrol in the car. My family supported me, buying side tables and spice racks. Believers would step in now and then, helping us out.

Holding onto the little money I had left, one day Sharon and I were sitting in the kitchen. Our baby and toddler were asleep in the bedroom. Looking out the kitchen window, I recognised a brother in the driveway coming towards our house. I had worked with him on previous jobs. He walked in with two shopping bags in his hands. He put the bags down, and we greeted each other. I told him to take a seat, and we all sat in the kitchen. Often, he would visit, and we would talk about the Lord.

We spoke about the Lord for a while, and then he got up to leave. I got up to see him out, realising he was not taking his shopping bags. I indicated to him about the bags, and he looked at me, pointing to the bags, and said, "Brother, this is for you." I was shocked and said, "Are you sure?" He nodded and smiled. I thanked him, surprised and grateful as we had been trusting GOD to make a way.

I saw him out, and he left. When I walked back into the house, we opened the bags. It was more than we expected. This is what happens when GOD blesses you. The bags contained everything we needed and more. We prayed, thanked GOD, and gave Him the glory for providing for us in our time of need. Even in our down moments, GOD was there to pick us up. Hebrews 13:5-6 says, "Let your conversation be without covetousness and be content with such things as ye have: for he hath said, I will never leave thee, nor forsake thee. So that we may boldly say, The Lord is my helper, and I will not fear what man shall do unto me."

For almost four years, we had been on the housing waiting list. I desperately needed a job to be able to purchase our family home when

Chapter 10

the right time came. Our current landlord felt the place was too small for our family, and we needed to find a bigger house to live in. GOD came through for me with a good job. Psalms 37:4 says, "Delight thyself also in the Lord, and he shall give thee the desires of thine heart."

Sharon's mum's friend opened her home for me and my family. It was a two-bedroom apartment. She lived alone and was glad to share her home with us. She said we could live with her while we waited. She was good to us, and GOD bless her for her kindness and understanding. We only lived with her for two months when the Lord came through for us. Sharon's mother had applied for an apartment in Wentworth, Durban. She was living in Johannesburg at the time. It was a two-bedroom, with a kitchen, lounge, toilet, and bathroom with hot water. My mother-in-law said we could occupy the apartment whilst we waited for our home.

I was in a good job, working away in Richards Bay. The money I earned allowed me to save for a deposit for our new home. I had good fellowship with my brethren on this job. One weekday, a supervisor invited me to his room to minister the word of GOD. He invited other people who were not believers. The brother playing the guitar was someone I had issues with in the past. In the world, we had fought and had disputes. Now, here we were in harmony. GOD works in mysterious ways that we cannot comprehend. At one stage in our lives, we both were lost, but here we were in a meeting doing GOD's work and winning souls for Jesus Christ.

A year later, I met up with two of the men who were in the meeting that night. One was now serving the Lord, and the other had started going to church. Being away from my family was not easy; I missed my wife and daughters. Sometimes, I would surprise my wife by randomly driving down to Durban, a two-hour drive, to be at home for the night. Early the next morning, I would leave for work and probably see my family again on the weekend.

During this time, my dad became very ill and was admitted to the hospital. I remember driving to the hospital from Richards Bay to see him. His words to me were, "Brian, you must visit your mother." It broke my heart to see him suffering, and the next morning, he had passed

SET FREE

away. It was a sad time for me, my mother, sisters, and brother. Sharon struggled with me working away, but there was no other option. She earnestly prayed for GOD to provide a home and for me to work locally so I could be home every day.

On Sundays, my sister and her husband would give my wife a lift to church when I was away. One Sunday, the minister was preaching, and he stopped and pointed to my wife, who was holding our baby asleep on her shoulder, with our toddler sitting on the chair next to her. He said, "Sister, I need to pray for you. I can see you are very burdened. Come to the front." Sharon shared this testimony with me.

My wife got up, took our toddler's hand, and walked to the front. His words to her were, "Where is your husband?" Sharon mentioned I was working away. He said, "We're going to pray right now in the name of Jesus for your husband to get a job locally so he can be home every day." They prayed for my wife and especially for me to find work locally. The apartment we lived in was surrounded by crime. One morning, I woke up to leave for work and found someone had stolen the wipers off the car. When the job I had ended, I made my way back home. The next day, Tuesday, there was a knock on the door. A friend of mine was passing by to let me know about a big job coming up in the Bayhead area, and they needed welders. I landed that job, and for the next four years, I had a stable job. GOD came through for me once more and provided me with local employment.

A few months later, my wife received a call congratulating us on our new home. We needed to come into the office, pay our deposit, and pick up the keys. GOD had prepared us for this, and I had been able to save money during all the years I worked locally. When my wife got the call, she ended it, fell on her knees, and cried before the Lord, unable to believe it. This was truly a miracle. We had waited patiently for almost two years, trusting GOD for this miracle. I was so excited—GOD truly answers prayers. He had come through again, providing us not with a rented home, but with our own home.

Philippians 4:19 says, "But my GOD shall supply all your need according to his riches in glory by Christ Jesus." One weekend, we

Chapter 10

took a drive, half an hour from Wentworth, to see our new home—a double-story duplex with three bedrooms, a bathroom, a lounge, and a separate toilet. There were 13 steps to the top level of the house and 28 steps leading to the front door. It was a nice house, and we were so appreciative to the Lord for blessing us with it. Our girls had grown, and they were excited too. They shared their own bedroom, and I had a study. I worked hard to make our home comfortable for my family. I plastered the walls, tiled all the floors, and installed ceiling fans in every room. I thank GOD for making the money available and giving me the strength to do all of this for my family.

The very first time we went to look at our new home, we couldn't see through the front lounge window because tall sugar cane branches had grown in the front yard. The backyard was the same. We came back with grass slashers, spades, and rakes to cut and clear all the overgrown bushes surrounding the area. This reminded me of my reformatory days, but it was nothing compared to the vast areas I worked on there. My wife was always by my side, trying to help with whatever she could. We were both so excited and thankful to GOD for our new home.

We didn't have a garage, so my Chevy was parked at the bottom of the stairway in the front yard. Early on a Sunday morning, while we were asleep, a loud bang woke me up. Looking out the bedroom window upstairs, which overlooked the front street and the road leading to the top of the hill, I saw a guy getting up from the ground next to my car. His motorbike was there, and he was trying to get back on it. He managed to get on and drove away. I watched him drive all the way to the top of the hill, where the road curved and there were more houses. He stopped at a house just around the curve.

I waited for daybreak. My car had been smashed, so I jumped into it and drove to the house where I saw him stop. Arriving there, I knocked on the door. A lady answered, and I asked her where the guy with the motorbike was. She said he was in the room and took me there. He was lying on the bed with his leg raised on a pillow. I told him I had seen him crash into my car with his motorbike. He apologised and said he was sorry. Seeing him lying on the bed with an injured leg, I felt sorry

SET FREE

for him. I told him not to worry; I would get my car fixed. I thank GOD for helping me see the situation differently. Had I not known GOD, my reactions would have been different. GOD had changed my life and placed compassion in my heart instead of anger towards others who did me wrong.

Part Two
Testimonies/Challenges

My daughters were invited to be flower girls at a family member's wedding. I planned with my wife to take them to Wentworth on Friday morning, and I would come through in the afternoon to pick her up. We had no car at the time as it was getting repaired. Our daughters would stay over at their grandmother's (my wife's mum) to be ready for the wedding in Wentworth the next day, Saturday. I picked my wife up from Wentworth, and we both boarded the first bus to the city. I had an umbrella and a pair of shoes in a shoebox in a bag. We got off the bus and held hands, making our way to the next bus stop.

Suddenly, four African men walked towards us, walked into us, and separated us. Three of the men got hold of me, each one with a dagger in his hand. At first, I was a little disoriented, but then I realised we were being robbed. It was Friday, my pay day, and I had my packet of wages in my front pocket. One of the men grabbed both my arms, the second man held a knife to my throat, and the third man flicked a knife in front of me.

He put the knife in his mouth and danced in front of me, demanding money and speaking in Zulu. Still holding onto the umbrella and the shoe bag, I felt a calmness come over me, realising the battle was not mine but the Lord's. Bending myself forward, I said, "I rebuke you in the name of the Lord Jesus Christ." My wife, unaware of the situation, had continued to walk until she heard my voice. She turned around, horrified to see I was being attacked by robbers. She called out loudly,

SET FREE

saying, "Satan, you are a liar!" The fourth man ran up to her, put a knife to her throat, and said, "Shut up, or I will kill you."

Continuing to call out, I said, "Satan, I rebuke you in the name of the Lord Jesus Christ." Saying it for the fifth time, they let me go. Sharon told me that from where she was standing, I seemed like a giant calling on the Lord, with the men hanging on to me. They let me go, ran a little distance away, and turned around to look at me with wide-open eyes. It seemed like they had seen something—angels, the supernatural? What was it that made them let me go and run away? Something they had seen had frightened them.

I stood for a while looking in their direction, then turned around and walked towards my wife. She was in shock and crying. I put my arm around her, comforting her. GOD had delivered us from this situation. It could have ended in tragedy; we could have been murdered that night. My pay was still in my pocket, and the umbrella and shoe bag were still in my hand. Only my wife's scarf had blown off her head. We walked away without a scratch from the knife. GOD provided a taxi for us. In the distance, we saw a parked taxi, and as we got closer, we saw that only the last two seats were available. My wife was still upset and shaken. I knew the taxi driver, who looked at me and asked what had happened. I told him my wife and I had been attacked by robbers, but I rebuked them in the name of the Lord Jesus Christ, and GOD delivered us from them.

The taxi driver said, "Truly, GOD is alive." He told me that last week, in the exact same place, a couple walking to the bus stop was attacked, and the man was stabbed to death. We jumped into the taxi and were safe. It took a long time for my wife to overcome her fear of African men. She had developed a phobia, but GOD delivered her, setting her free.

When we arrived home, inside the house, I took my wife's hand, and we got on our knees at the lounge coffee table. We thanked GOD for His protection and for delivering us that night. I was grateful my daughters were not with us at the time. I recalled a prayer from some time ago, asking GOD to show me He was with me. This experience was

Chapter 10

a lesson for me: GOD is always with us, and we need to be careful what we ask for. We must believe and trust in Him always. This testimony has always affirmed to me that GOD is real, alive, and His angels are encamped around us. Psalm 91:11 says, "For He shall give His angels charge over thee, to keep thee in all thy ways." Psalms 34:7 says, "The angel of the Lord encampeth round about them that fear Him, and delivereth them." GOD is so good.

One day, my wife had gone with our daughters to Wentworth to visit. When she got off the bus and walked up the stairs, she was surprised to find the front door open. She walked into the house, and the kitchen door was wide open too. She walked into the kitchen and saw that the kettle and the toaster were missing. She panicked a little, thinking the intruder was still in the house, probably upstairs. She walked up the stairs.

She peeped into the study; all the books were thrown down from the shelf. In the children's bedroom, all the drawers were on the floor along with their clothes. Walking into the main room, she thought the culprit might be there, but there was no one. Instead, all the clothes had been pulled out of the wardrobes, and Bibles were on the floor. My wife saw a very strange thing: a full pay packet, my wages, was lying untouched in a drawer on the floor. It was as if something had disturbed the intruder. Later, we noticed my wife's hair dryer was missing. This robber only stole electrical equipment. GOD had protected our home, and the items lost could be replaced.

I lost my job again and prayerfully trusted GOD to make a way. With my kind of trade, this was normal; our jobs always came to an end. Financially, things started to get a little tough. I was out looking for work, and my wife always prayed and asked GOD to come through for us, and He always did. One day, she was sitting on the lawn, waiting for the postman to arrive.

The postman came, and she prayed, "Please, Lord, today put a letter into our postbox." She stood there watching, and he really did pop mail into the postbox. She walked down the stairs to get the mail. Taking the mail, she saw on the envelope in bold letters: "The Receiver of

SET FREE

Revenue," meaning it was from the tax office. It was either we owed them, or they owed us. My wife opened the letter and was shocked to see that money was due to us. She said, "Thank you, Lord, but this is not enough to cover our bills."

The next day, the postman came by and popped a letter into the postbox. My wife didn't think much of it since she had received their letter yesterday. She took the letter out of the postbox and saw "Receiver of Revenue" written on the envelope again. She thought this time we would owe them. Opening the envelope and reading the letter, she found that more money was due to us. Unbelievably, GOD had financially made a way for us. This was very real to me, and my faith was uplifted. I always knew in His time He would come through for me and my family. He is a prayer-answering GOD.

We were now mobile, and I drove my wife to see her friend in Wentworth. I stayed in the car while she went to see her friend in the apartment. A friend I had known before I came to Christ, before I was born again, came around the corner. Seeing me from a distance, he smiled and asked if I was still saved. I smiled back and said, "Yes, I am still saved." I thought to myself that he was hoping I would say no, thinking we could be together again. GOD had really changed my life; there was nothing in me that desired to be in the world again. I didn't want to live an unGODly life. Nothing was going to deter my faith, especially after GOD revealed Himself to me in so many marvellous ways.

GOD showed me His hand on me and my family, whom I loved dearly. My wife loved the LORD and was a tower of strength to me. When I think back to how we met, there was just one house that separated us from her apartment. GOD brought her right to me, to come and live in our neighbourhood. Proverbs 18:22 says, "Whoso findeth a wife findeth a good thing and obtaineth favour of the Lord."

We had a small fellowship in the next suburb where we lived. We had no car. The Chevy '41 I had for many years had been smashed into a pole by a company repairing my car. The car was driven by a coworker, and the brakes had failed, smashing my Chevy. A brother I knew from another fellowship came to visit me one evening. He came with another

Chapter 10

brother, driving a red Pulsar. He walked into our home and presented me with a car logbook in my name. I opened the logbook and saw my name. He smiled, looked at me, and said, "It's for you, brother. The car is yours. I bought this car for you."

My brother-in-law and sister would come all the way from Wentworth. He would preach in our fellowship. I gave them the car to use as a form of transport so on Sundays they could come and be a blessing to the people in the fellowship. GOD had blessed me, and I felt the need to bless others. GOD made a way for me and provided me with my next job.

Whenever I would come home after looking for work with the good news that I would be starting a new job soon, it was a moment of excitement for both of us. She would hug me, and we would just hold each other. She would say to me, "I have been praying all day for you." My trade always required a weld test, and if you did not pass the test, there was no job. For some reason, even in my welding tests, GOD always saw me through. It became challenging at times, but I would always pray before I started my test and pass it.

On Sundays, I would take a bus to the end of our suburb and then walk about 2 km to the next suburb. We loved the Lord and looked forward to being in His presence. My wife was pregnant with our third child, and we were trusting GOD for a boy. During this time, I became ill. One night, I woke up in pain near my heart. I curled up, feeling tremendous pain, and did not know what to do. I called out to my wife. She got out of bed, switched on the light, and checked on me, worriedly saying, "Brian." I was shrivelled up on the bed, moaning and groaning. She said I looked pale and was sweating. She prayed for me, and the pain subsided. It felt like it could have been a heart attack because the pain was so severe around my heart.

The next day, my wife and I went to the doctor. He checked my heart and blood pressure and had me do some exercises. He looked at me and said that my heart was in good shape. He told me not to worry and said it could have just been a muscle spasm. I said, "Thank you, Lord," what a relief. Another time, I fell ill with a high fever and was

SET FREE

continuously vomiting. All through the night, my wife got some towels and a basin of water and sponged me, making sure to keep the fever down. It was hectic for her because she was pregnant, but she wanted to make me comfortable and control the temperature. In the morning, she called the doctor to check on me. He was surprised to see that she was pregnant but still able to take care of me. I had a gastro virus, and he prescribed medication. He told me I was in good hands and that my wife had done a good job. She always said it was only GOD giving her the strength and leading her to do the right thing for me. The doctor said that if the fever had not been controlled, I would have been hospitalised. Isaiah 53:5 says, "But he was wounded for our transgressions, he was bruised for our iniquities: the chastisement of our peace was upon him; and with his stripes we are healed."

Working on an oil rig in the Bayhead area on a Saturday was not the norm, but when we were busy, we were asked to work on weekends. We worked with a trade assistant to help with the job, and on this particular day, I needed one. I spoke to the supervisor, who mentioned that one of the welders was absent, so his trade assistant could work with me. He was a young Zulu guy who was on drugs at the time. I started to witness to him about the Lord Jesus Christ. I always carried my New Testament pocket bible in the top pocket of my work overalls. Taking my Bible out, I began talking to him. He asked me if what I was saying was true and if it was in the Bible. I answered yes, and I noticed tears starting to roll down his cheeks. He said, "Brian, I want to serve the Lord." I continued to share the word of GOD with him. Although he primarily spoke Zulu and I knew only a little Zulu and he spoke a bit of English, we managed to communicate. From that day onwards, every time he had the opportunity to work with me, I would witness to him.

He was so excited about giving his life to Christ that he started to witness to the other Zulu men he worked with. He was no longer on drugs; he had given them up. His friends did not want to believe him when he mentioned he was serving GOD. He insisted they come and ask me, and I confirmed that Sandile was indeed serving the Lord. Our job came to an end, and we went our separate ways. A few months

Chapter 10

later, I had started another job. One morning, after a night shift, I saw Sandile. He could have been working at a company nearby. I stopped my car; he was smiling and so excited to see me. He jumped in, and I took him home to my house. I was mobile again, having bought a BMW at a good price from a dealer. When we got home, my wife made him a cup of tea. We sat in the lounge, having tea together. He asked if I could take him home, which was in the next African township called Kwa Mashu. Driving into this area with a BMW was dangerous due to the high risk of hijacking, crime, and robbery.

I went to the kitchen to tell my wife. I could see the worried look on her face. She said, "Brian, you cannot go there; it's too dangerous." Sandile heard my wife and called out from the lounge, "Sister, you must learn to trust GOD." This was a challenge. I realised that I had led him to Christ, and now I had to prove to him that I trusted GOD to take care of me no matter what. I hugged my wife, telling her not to worry and that GOD would protect me. I assured her that I would be okay, although I could see she was still worried. I drove Sandile to his house. He lived on the top of a hill in a small corrugated iron house. I thought I would just drop him off and drive away, but he wanted me to come to the house, meet his family, and pray before I left. I had to leave my car parked on a dead-end road at the bottom of the hill. We walked towards his house, and he pointed to a taxi rank not far away, mentioning that there had been a shoot-out there the previous day. We got to his house, where he introduced me to his family. Before I left, we prayed together.

After I finished praying, I thought he would walk me down to my car. Instead, he stood at the door with his family, saying, "Thanks, Brian, for bringing me home." I walked alone to my car and drove off. GOD was good; I was safe, and I still had my car. Nothing had happened; GOD had protected me. As 2 Thessalonians 3:3 says, "But the Lord is faithful, who shall establish you from evil." My wife was so excited to see me, and I saw the sigh of relief on her face. She walked towards me, hugged me, and said, "Brian, I was so worried about you. I prayed for you from the time you left." A few years passed, and I had not seen Sandile since.

SET FREE

I attended a big convention, a combined service with other churches. It was a huge gathering at a stadium with crowds of people. Sitting in the stadium with my family, we watched some church choir groups perform on stage, singing songs to the glory of GOD. When the group finished their item, I heard the convenor say, "Now we would like to have Pastor Sandile and his church come to the stage to sing unto the Lord." It did not cross my mind that this was the same Sandile I had witnessed to a few years ago. To my surprise, I looked towards the stage, and there he was, walking onto the stage with his church.

My wife recognised him too and was equally surprised. After the service, as people were leaving and making their way to the car park, I saw Sandile and waved to him. When he saw me, he was so excited, repeatedly calling my name as he walked towards me. He introduced me to the members of his fellowship as his pastor, repeatedly saying, "This is my pastor." It was so good to see him again and witness what GOD had done in his life. I felt encouraged to see GOD changing people's lives.

Chapter 11
GOD Blessed Me

Continuing to serve GOD with my family, my wife became a Sunday school teacher at the fellowship, and I, along with other brethren, would minister the word of GOD on Sunday mornings. My wife was in her 26th week of her pregnancy, and we trusted GOD, already having chosen a name. By faith, we both believed it was going to be a boy. I liked the biblical name Hosea.

Living in a double-story home, it became difficult for my pregnant wife. There were thirteen steps leading to the bathroom downstairs. One night, needing the bathroom, she climbed out of bed and walked barefoot to the steps leading downstairs. On the second step, she stepped onto a live gecko, which made a squeaky noise. She lost her balance and rolled down the remaining eleven steps. I heard a thud and a moan, jumped out of bed to check, and switched on the light at the top of the stairs. I was shocked to see my wife lying at the bottom of the steps, groaning. I ran down the steps towards her, saying, "Sharon, what happened? Oh no."

I picked her up in my arms, asking, "Sharon, are you okay?" I put her down on the couch. She was conscious and could talk. All she said was, "My leg, my ankle, it hurts." I looked at her ankle, and it was swollen and blue. I applied a cold compress. She was in tremendous pain.

This was such a difficult situation for me at the time. I couldn't leave my wife and go to work, especially with her in this condition. I had just started a new job, and since it wasn't a long-term position, staying away from work could get me fired. Financially, we needed the money, so this

SET FREE

was a hard decision to make. My wife couldn't be left alone with our two daughters, who needed to be taken care of and taken to school.

I called my mother-in-law and asked her to please come over and help with my daughters. She gladly agreed, taking two buses to get to our house. I felt bad about leaving my wife, but I was in a difficult situation. My mother-in-law got the girls ready for school and suggested taking my wife to the medical centre for an x-ray to check if the baby was okay. My wife had an x-ray done on her ankle; she couldn't walk and had to hop along. Her ankle was fractured, and the tendon was torn. Fortunately, the baby was fine and still moving as normal. My mother-in-law stayed with my wife to help. GOD bless her; she had always been a great help, supportive and willing to assist whenever she could.

Two weeks later, in the 28th week, my wife's waters ruptured, but she felt no pain. This was unexpected. I helped her pack a bag and took her to the hospital, as it was the safest place for her at that time. My daughters stayed with my mother-in-law. At the hospital, my wife explained that her waters had ruptured prematurely at 28 weeks. The nurse assured me that my wife was safe and that I should leave so they could admit her and take care of things.

The next day, while I was at work, my wife called me. She told me the hospital had done nothing for her and that she had to walk quite a distance to make the call. I advised her to go back to the ward and rest. She hadn't gone into labour yet, and the hospital was just monitoring her condition.

That night, she went into labour. The room was set up with an incubator, but my wife didn't have a good feeling about this and started to pray. Her labour was intense, and she tried walking to help herself, but the nurse suggested she stay in bed because her waters had already ruptured. My wife felt the staff were too slow in deciding what was best for her and the baby. The painful contractions grew stronger and lasted longer. My wife told me how she felt the presence of GOD and began to pray for our baby, dedicating him to the Lord. She asked GOD to help her through this painful ordeal.

Chapter 11

Suddenly, nurses and a few doctors walked into the room and stood around her bed, looking worried. I was praying for her too, even though I couldn't be there; I was at home with our daughters. It was a difficult time for me.

Our families lived in Wentworth, which was quite far and inconvenient to reach. As the nurses and doctors tried to assure her that everything would be alright, complications started to set in. She could bear the pain, but this type of pain and suffering was unbearable. Her tummy became rock hard, intensifying the pain, and she struggled to breathe. Both she and our baby were connected to heart monitors. Looking up and struggling with herself, she could see the beats on the screen's graph. The doctor tried to examine her and mentioned that the baby was going into distress. My wife teared up, continuing to pray.

The baby's heartbeats on the monitor started to fade away until they disappeared completely. Hosea did not make it. The doctor looked at my wife, held her hand, and said he was sorry, explaining the next step to deliver our unborn baby. They sedated my wife, and within five minutes, she gave birth to our son. Drowsy from the medication, everything became a blur, and she wasn't in the right frame of mind. The nurse wrapped our baby and gently tried to hand him to my wife, but she was too sedated. I could have lost my wife, the love of my life, but GOD took care of her during the storm and saw her through.

At 4:30 am, I was awake praying when I heard a knock on the door. My sister and her husband came to break the news to me. My wife was still heavily sedated, and they were there to take me to the hospital to see my wife and baby. I slowly walked up the stairs in shock while they waited downstairs. I walked into my bedroom, shaken and emotional. A numb and empty feeling came over me as I cried and wondered why this was happening. I was serving the Lord and loved Him with all my heart. I was devastated.

We dropped my daughters at their grandmother's in Wentworth, and my sister and her husband drove me to the hospital. Still shaken upon arrival, I walked into the room where my wife was, and we just held each other and cried. A nurse came and asked if I would like to see the baby. I said yes. She took me to a crib standing against a wall, and there he was, our baby boy, wrapped up as if he were just sleeping. A great sadness came over me. I had two daughters, and now the son I desired was taken away from me. Despite this, my faith in GOD did not waver. I knew He was in control and knew what was best for our lives.

My sister, who was strong in her faith, was a real pillar and tower of strength to my wife. She took care of her at the hospital, ensuring my wife was comfortable. When the nurses wheeled my wife into the ward, my sister sat at her bedside and said, "Sharry, I am here. You have a rest, try to sleep. When you wake up, I will still be here." GOD bless my sister D's and her husband for being there during this difficult time in our lives. My wife had lost a significant amount of blood during childbirth. The doctors attending to her recommended a blood transfusion the next day. They would first check and do tests to see if it was needed before proceeding with the transfusion. We prayed earnestly for this not to be necessary and trusted GOD to make a way. My wife prayed, fearing an allergic reaction or a transmitted virus. The next morning, the doctors did their rounds, tested my wife, and said there was no need for a transfusion; she was fine. Thank you, Lord, I was grateful.

It took my wife a while to recover. She was prescribed strong antibiotics for an extended period. I trusted GOD to give her strength and help her overcome this ordeal. Some nights, she would wake up and cry about our baby. I would hold her in my arms and comfort her, telling her that Hosea is with the Lord and that one day we will see him on the other side. It broke my heart to see her this way; she needed me.

One of the sisters from the church came to live with us to help my wife during this time. She was a blessing, helping with my daughters, cooking meals, and taking care of the home. GOD bless her. After three months, GOD had removed my wife's complexes, and she wanted to go to church. There, she testified how GOD had made a way for her. I knew in my heart that GOD had restored her and helped her overcome. I still

Chapter 11

dwell on this, but I know one day I will see my boy Hosea on the other side. April 30, 1987, is the day we always remember when our little boy went home to be with the Lord. Every year, my wife remembers this day; it will never be erased from our lives.

My wife decided to take up dressmaking lessons in the city while our daughters attended school. My mum blessed her with a Singer Vintage sewing machine, which was special. In my father's working days, he had done a building job for his boss, who, feeling blessed and happy with the job, gave him the sewing machine. My mother, who was also a dressmaker, upgraded to a more modern machine and passed the Singer Vintage to my wife. This machine was a real blessing to us. My wife put it to good use. When we moved into our own home, she sewed curtains, couch covers, pillowcases, duvet covers, and the most beautiful dresses for herself and our daughters. She could read a dress pattern and spent a lot of time sewing. It was therapeutic for her after all she had been through. She could also mend my work overalls and jeans. GOD blessed her with a gift.

We continued to serve the Lord with all our hearts. We started going to another fellowship, a bigger church. My wife and I were very active there. On Friday nights, I would take my family to band practice, an evening with the musicians, practicing songs, and enjoying good fellowship, cake, and tea. I became a song leader at the church services on Sunday, and my wife was a lead singer in the church band. On Saturday mornings, we would have open-air meetings where the band would set up, and the pastor would evangelise to crowds of people hungry to hear the word of GOD. It was a real blessing and encouragement for me on this journey with my fellow brothers and sisters.

Sometimes my jobs were far out, and I would not be around. My wife faithfully attended church with our children, never missing a service. Several years later, my wife woke up and shared a dream with me. She dreamt that we had a son. In her dream, he looked like a three-year-old boy running towards her with open arms, saying, "Mummy, catch me." As she bent forward, opening her arms to catch him, he resembled her.

SET FREE

Catching him, she threw him up in the air. The colour of his hair looked the same as hers. My wife said, "Brian, I believe in my heart GOD is going to bless us with a son." I believe by faith he confirmed it with this dream. Two months later, my wife conceived. She believed it was a boy and did not want to know the gender of the child because GOD had already told her. She was excited and everything she purchased for the baby was blue. She always mentioned him, knitting blue booties and a cap. Not once did she doubt but had faith that GOD was giving us a baby boy.

While she was still pregnant, a job came up for me in Cape Town. It was the beginning of December, and I had to go away. In early January, I was back home and started another job in the Bayhead area, closer to home. My wife was well overdue at 42 weeks when the gynaecologist suggested induced labour. On January 25, 1991, our baby boy was born, and my job contract ended the same day. Excited, GOD had blessed me with a son; a job did not matter at the time.

What a blessing! GOD had given us our heart's desire. During his developing months, our baby boy became very ill at times. He was just a year old when he had his tonsils removed, causing us a lot of grief, high temperatures, and sleepless nights. If his fever was not controlled, it would lead to a convulsion. He had these a few times. One day, at the tender age of three, he woke up from his sleep and made his way down the stairs. Suddenly, when he reached the end of the steps, he zoned out, staring at one spot. He went into a stiff position, and a convulsion followed.

During this time, I was working locally at home. My wife rang me at work, telling me to come quickly as the doctor was on his way to the house; our boy was sick. Some of the neighbours came over to the house, hearing the commotion. My eldest daughter was 12 or 13 years old. My wife was very weary at this stage, taking care of a sick baby. She walked upstairs, stood by the wardrobe door, and sobbed. My daughter comforted her, saying, "It's going to be okay, Mummy. Don't cry." The doctor arrived, and my boy lay on the couch, motionless.

Chapter 11

Some of the neighbours in the house started to cry. The doctor told my wife the baby's pulse was very faint, and we needed to get him to the hospital as soon as possible. I got into my car and drove home as fast as I could. Arriving home, I ran down the driveway and entered the lounge. I asked the doctor to please move aside. I knelt next to my boy, holding him in my arms, and prayed earnestly for him, trusting GOD. My wife stood close by, crying and praying. Matthew 18:20 says, "For where two or three are gathered together in my name, there am I in the midst." I believed GOD with all my heart and trusted him. By faith, he would raise my son up. Suddenly, my son sat up and said, "Daddy." I felt unspeakable joy. GOD had made a way where there seemed to be no way. The neighbours, doctor, my wife, my daughter, and I witnessed the power of GOD.

We dressed my son and took him to the hospital. The fever had disappeared, and he was well again. He got ill again during a Sunday service, but for some reason, GOD proved himself again. He is a mighty GOD. He healed and delivered my son Seth.

I recall when my son was eight years old; my sister had given us a hamster. It was a Sunday afternoon, and my family and I had just returned from church. We were living in an apartment at the time. My wife walked with our children to the apartment while I stayed outside to chat with one of the brethren. We lived on the first floor, and I was standing on the ground floor talking.

While still in conversation with this brother, I heard my son call out to me. He said, "Dad, the hamster has fallen out of the cage, and it's dead." I excused myself and went to see what was happening. Before coming to tell me about the hamster, my son had worriedly picked it up, put it back in the cage, and then decided to come and inform me. The drop from the cage to the floor was one meter high. I investigated the cage and saw the hamster lying there motionless.

Placing my hands on the hamster, I began to pray for it. My son stood close by, watching. As I continued to pray in the name of the Lord Jesus Christ, I felt a movement under my hands. The hamster got up and started running around the cage. I wanted my son to witness the power of GOD, to have faith, and to believe in GOD. My son was so excited to see the hamster alive. Truly, GOD is alive.

My son did not enjoy academics; his preference was technical work, much like his dad. He was good at school sports and always participated. He chose to become a welder. I am not being biased because he is my son, but from a professional welder's perspective, he is excellent. It's in his genes; he owns his own engineering company and is thriving in his business. He is settled and married.

Years later, my wife became pregnant with our fifth child, a bubbly little baby girl. I called her a chubby checker. I witnessed her birth, and she looked just like her mother. She's all grown up now, having studied and become an early childhood educator with a diploma. She also studied justice studies in Australia, earning a diploma. Photography is her highlight, she enjoys baking bread, and she is married.

My eldest daughter is an achiever, always putting herself out there and taking on challenges with a very positive mindset. She has her own business related to hospitality, is hardworking, loves people, and makes a good host and entertainer. She is married.

My second daughter is also an achiever, not allowing anything to beat her. She studied and became an occupational therapist. She enjoys her job, especially working in the stroke ward with the older generation, showing them compassion. GOD has blessed our children with good spouses, and they love the Lord Jesus Christ. We have also been blessed with seven grandchildren. Our eldest grandson is married, and GOD has blessed him with a GOD-fearing wife, bringing us to eight grandchildren.

GOD has given me this beautiful family. My wife and I have earnestly prayed and invested in our children's spiritual lives, praying for them daily, providing GODly counsel, asking GOD for wisdom and direction, and showing love. The outcome is that they love GOD. For this, I can say, "Thank you, Lord, for blessing me."

Chapter 12
Many Places/Countries

We continued to live in our home and serve the Lord. Depending on my job situation, my finances fluctuated, influencing how long my jobs lasted. I tried to make our home as comfortable as possible for my family. I had a driveway done and fully fenced our backyard, making it safe for the children. I also made and welded my own driveway gate. We could afford a cleaner and a gardener to help out at home, which was necessary as our family had grown, and my wife needed the help.

A job opportunity arose in Angola, specifically in Cabinda, 85 kilometres out at sea on an oil rig. Everything was safe but it was a risk. I made this trip once a month. South Africa was having issues with Angola at the time. On one of my work trips flying from South Africa to Angola, almost two hundred men were on board. The route was from South Africa, stopping in Angola to refuel before flying to Cabinda, where we would take a ferry to the oil rig.

We landed in Angola, and the plane switched off completely, which seemed unusual. Suddenly, I saw the pilot, co-pilot, and the air hostess exiting the plane. Before they left, they told us all to remain seated. After a few minutes, a local from the airport shouted that we all needed to get off the plane. We exited the plane and were directed into the departure area of the airport. The air conditioning was not working, and it was very hot inside the building. As I started to perspire, the men began complaining about the heat. After a while, we realised we were being hijacked. Angola demanded a ransom

SET FREE

from South Africa and only then would the plane be released to fly to Cabinda.

The negotiation between Angola and South Africa took a very long time. We waited for several hours. Finally, everything settled, and we were able to fly to Cabinda. South African Airways stopped flying to Angola and handed the contract to Zambia Airlines. We then started to use Zambia Airlines to fly to Angola for work.

One day, I was fast asleep on the flotel, a five-story accommodation out at sea. The anchors holding the flotel became loose, and it started drifting further out to sea. I woke up, got dressed for work, and came out of my room. My friend stood nearby and asked, "Brian, where are you going? Can you see the oil rig?"

Usually, from our accommodation, I could see the oil rig, but when I stood at the rails, there was no oil rig in sight. He told me that throughout the night, the flotel had been drifting. It could take another whole day for the tugs to pull us back to where we needed to be anchored and positioned.

We would have church meetings on the oil rig. I had the opportunity to witness to a Congolese man, and he was very excited about the Lord. When we parted, I promised him I would send him a Bible and some Christian literature. I posted them to him, but the books were returned to us because a war was taking place in the Congo, and part of the post office was burned down.

I worked on the oil rig job for four months before resigning and getting a job closer to home. The money was good, and I was able to provide for my family, meeting our needs. I missed my family, and being away from them was not easy. My trade took me to many places: Cape Town, Johannesburg, and other towns in South Africa. I also worked in America for six months, including New Orleans, West Virginia, and American Samoa, where I helped build a hot fire training facility at the airport. A year later, American Samoa was hit by a tsunami, and I thank the Lord I was not working there at the time. GOD protected me.

I have lived and worked in three countries: South Africa, New Zealand, and Australia. GOD has been with me throughout my time in

CHAPTER 12

these countries. I have met and witnessed to brethren from different walks of life. We lived in Newlands East for a decade and then decided to venture out. We sold our home and moved to the Bluff, to a house near the beach. My family loved it, and seeing them happy made me happy. Walking down the pathway to the beach brought back childhood memories of the time I went to the beach with my friends and cut my foot. Over time, many changes had taken place, including the construction of steps to walk down to the beach. We lived in this area for two years.

By then, we owned a Ford Bantam bakkie (Ute), which I had purchased from my father-in-law. He owned a car sale and shipping company, importing goods from India. He would provide my wife with stock to sell at a flea market in Durban, South Africa. On Saturday mornings, my wife and I would load the car with stock, and our children, and head to the Point Waterfront market. I would help my wife set up, and my two eldest daughters would take charge. My wife would drive me to work with our two younger children and then return to the flea market for the day. After work, she would pick me up, and we would help her load the bakkie, pack up, and head home.

The stock included dresses, shirts, skirts, crockery sets, t-shirts, umbrellas, beach tongs, and even curry powder. My wife would pick up all this stock from his warehouse in Jacobs. I purchased clothing rails, and our home looked like a shop. Sometimes, I would take stock to work and show the men there. Many of them made appointments for us to come to their homes, and they would buy from us. I started to feel like a salesman at work, even the storeman would keep stock for me. Despite this, I did not allow the business to interfere with my spiritual life and still attended church on Sundays with my family.

Sometimes, my mother-in-law would help if our maid, Dudu, could not be there. Dudu was sincere and trustworthy. The children loved being around her and enjoyed her company. She was a great help to my wife with house cleaning, looking after the children, and working at the flea market.

SET FREE

Many trials came our way, but we stood firm and strong in the Lord. We continued with the flea market for six months and then stopped. It was beneficial, as my father-in-law only wanted a small profit. The season ended, and we trusted that GOD was in control.

During our stay on the Bluff, my eldest daughter was in a severe accident. We had the youth over at our house, and my daughter decided to take her friends for ice cream at Milky Lane. Having her driver's licence, I felt comfortable allowing her to drive our Ford Bantam bakkie. There were eleven of them in the bakkie, three in the front and eight in the back. My son cried because he wanted to go with them, but I said only the older children were going. My daughter left with the youth, and within ten minutes, one of them came running into the house with blood all over his hands. He had jumped out of the moving bakkie. The vehicle was too heavy at the back, causing it to swerve and topple over, rolling down into the bushes.

My wife and I rushed to the scene of the accident. We saw bodies lying scattered on the grass, some moaning and groaning. The children were badly hurt; it was a distressing sight. My other daughter, out of shock, ran all the way to St Monica's home nearby. The bakkie had rolled quite far down the bank into the bush. The fire brigade arrived and assisted in removing the bakkie. I found myself going to each child, screaming out in pain, praying for them and asking the Lord to touch them. It was a harrowing experience. Two ambulances arrived, and my nephew, who was a doctor, happened to be taking a Sunday drive with his family along the same road, unaware of what lay ahead. GOD's timing was perfect. He came across the accident and stopped to check it out, horrified to find his cousins and church friends involved. He was able to assist.

My wife and I felt responsible for all these children. It was our bakkie and our daughter. One of the boys, the pastor's son, was in a bad condition. The pastor came to the scene of the accident. Seeing him weep over his son and praying, I realised that only GOD could make a way. We needed Him now more than ever.

Chapter 12

My daughter was lying in the bush. I remember praying for her too. She started to feel sleepy, and all I could hear was the nurse saying, "Stay with me, talk to me, try not to sleep." Seeing all this was overwhelming, and I worried if everyone was going to make it, if everyone would come out of this. It was a tough trial, and we prayed earnestly. I asked myself how I would live my life if one of the children didn't make it. I trusted GOD for complete healing for the pastor's son, who was worse off than the others.

My wife and I visited the hospital to see him. The congregation was there every night, visiting and praying. We felt awful, burdened with guilt. Our pastor visited us the next morning at 5:30 am with the assistant pastor, whose sons were also in the accident. They reassured us, saying they had nothing against us, that we were all family, and that together we would trust GOD for all the children. It was such a relief for my wife and me to hear this, and we felt supported by our brothers and sisters. The whole church prayed, and GOD came through. A year later, the eleven friends, including my daughters, stood on stage and testified about the goodness of GOD. My daughter, who drove the bakkie on the day of the accident, mentioned that the bakkie struggled up the hill due to the weight at the back.

As she reached the top of the hill, the steering wheel started spinning on its own. She tried to grab the steering wheel, but it continued spinning very fast. The bakkie hit the curb and lost control, rolling down a steep bush. A strange thing happened while the bakkie was rolling—she saw herself as a little girl rolling down a green grassy hill. After hopping out of the car, she, suffering from a concussion, walked toward the top of the hill. People who knew my wife and me asked her where her parents were. Severely concussed, she said we were in the bakkie, but we were actually at home.

A year later, the church had a thanksgiving service, thanking the Lord for what He had done. All eleven of them stood on the stage, healed and well. They survived and sang the song "AFTER ALL I'VE BEEN THROUGH, I STILL HAVE JOY." My wife and I were overjoyed. Once

SET FREE

again, GOD proved His love for us, always seeing us through the storms and setting us free from the burdens that weighed us down.

Leaving South Africa to come to New Zealand was not an easy decision. My mother lived in Wentworth, in the same area, in the same house where I had grown up as a little boy. My brother was married, and his wife and two sons lived with my mother. My sisters, with their families, still lived in the country. In May 2003, a cousin visited from Australia. We had a wall figurine on the front wall of the house, a Mexican man asleep with a hat over his head. Jokingly, he said, "Brian, how long are you going to sleep like this amigo on the wall? Come overseas; it's better for you and your family." South Africa was changing fast; crime was rampant, and it was not safe where we were living. We had an American pit bull at the time—a real family dog who did his duty and protected our home. I had bought a home in Woodlands, my second time buying a home. My eldest daughter worked at a medical centre, so we used her little red Uno to get around. My transport to work was the taxis, which were very unsafe. I thought of my family and prayed daily for GOD to make a way for us.

At the time, I was in a permanent job working for Umgeni Water. Two opportunities came up for me: a business opportunity to go into business with my ex-boss, a Frenchman, and a job opportunity in New Zealand. This was not an easy decision, and I needed wisdom from GOD to make the right choice. I told my wife that we were both going to earnestly pray and ask GOD to lead us and make a way for us. The next morning at 5:30 am, we humbly knelt before the Lord, making our requests and decisions known. Financially, I was not prepared to pay for a ticket to New Zealand.

Later that afternoon, I received an email stating that my ticket to New Zealand would be paid for. I felt a load lift off my shoulders, and I knew GOD was in the midst, making a way for me. I turned down the offer from my ex-boss, who said to come and see him before I went overseas. My ticket was sent to me, and in September 2003, the same year my cousin had visited me and made the joke about going overseas, I prepared to leave.

Chapter 12

On September 5, 2003, I flew out of South Africa. It was hard leaving my family behind. We had put our home up for sale, and many other things needed to be sorted out. My stopover from Durban, South Africa, was in Hong Kong. I safely arrived in Hong Kong, with no idea of the challenges I would face. To me, this was another journey for work, with my family following later. I went through customs, sorted out my boarding pass for the next flight to New Zealand, and waited at the boarding gate.

Soon, a ground attendant walked towards me and asked to see my boarding pass and passport. I handed my documents to her. She looked at them, looked at me, and told me to come with her. She took me to an airline official, who took my boarding pass and tore it up in front of me. He said I needed to go back to South African Airlines to fly back to South Africa. Confused, I asked him why. He looked at me and said, "Do you have enough funds to go to New Zealand?" I said yes, but I was unaware that a certain amount was required to enter New Zealand. I explained that I had money on me and could withdraw more from the ATM, but my daily limit of 1000 rand was going to complicate things. The time difference didn't help either.

I went back to the official to explain, but he looked at me and walked away. So, I stood there, unable to board the flight to New Zealand because my boarding pass was torn. Due to all the drama, I missed the flight. I called my wife and explained what had happened at the Hong Kong airport. She listened calmly and said, "Brian, don't go anywhere. Wait there, we're going to pray about this." Later, my wife explained that she had gathered the children together, told them to stand in a circle, and explained the situation. She told them, "Daddy is having problems at the Hong Kong Airport. The officials want him to fly back to South Africa." She then told the children, "We are not accepting any negativity. Instead, we are going to desperately pray and ask GOD to make a way for Daddy to go to New Zealand. Today, we are going to trust GOD with all our hearts."

She prayed with all her heart, alongside our children, like never before. GOD led her to call her sister in Australia and explain the

SET FREE

situation. Due to the time difference, her sister called throughout the night trying to arrange help. My wife didn't sleep that night, taking her sister's calls. As it started to get late, I walked over to South African Airways to tell them not to put my luggage through; I was not going back to South Africa and would be booking into a hotel. I went through Hong Kong immigration, and they stamped my passport for a three-month stay. I walked out of the airport and noticed the Hong Kong airport hotel. I booked a room, received my keys, and made my way to my room. I thought to myself, at least I have accommodation for the night. I knelt at the bedside and started to pray. While praying, the phone rang. It was my sister-in-law, who had tracked me down and found me at the hotel. She told me she was going to get in touch with someone in Hong Kong and would call me back. I continued to pray and trust GOD.

Later, my sister-in-law called again, saying she had contacted some believers in Hong Kong who would come to the hotel to see me the next day. She told me that one of the brethren would be holding a book in his hand. I slept through the night and went to get breakfast in the morning, sitting on a big open patio. A Chinese man walked past holding up a placard with my name written in big letters. I thought to myself, what now, am I in trouble? Reluctantly, I took my time before saying I was Brian, not knowing what to expect. Eventually, I raised my hand to indicate I was Brian. The man put his hand out for me to follow him. I got up from the chair and walked with him. He pointed to the phone on the table, picked it up, answered it, and then handed it to me. I answered and heard my wife's voice on the other end. She was worried about me and asked how I was. It was so comforting to hear her voice. She told me to stay where I was because the brethren would be coming to see me soon. My wife was in contact with her sister, and they both knew where I was and could now reach me.

While sitting there, I noticed two men walking towards me, one holding a book in his hand. They were from a church in Hong Kong. They recognised me and headed straight in my direction, smiling. We introduced ourselves, and due to our shared Christian fellowship, we talked about the Lord. They were fully aware of my situation and handed me

Chapter 12

cash in a bag. Before departing, they gave me their contact details in case I needed to reach them. I made my way back to the airport and checked the departure board for a flight to New Zealand. I noticed a flight at 4 pm with Air New Zealand, but it was cancelled. I couldn't get a flight to New Zealand. I walked to another airline, but they said I must book with Air New Zealand for help. I was stuck and couldn't fly out. As it started getting late, I sat on a bench, feeling weary. I prayed and asked GOD to make a way, still trusting Him. My mind was already made up; I was not going back to South Africa.

When the brethren came to see me earlier, they mentioned that I should not book into a hotel at the airport as it was very expensive. They offered to take me to a cheaper accommodation if I contacted them. Now it was late, and the shops in the airport started to close. The number of people dwindled, and a soldier and a policeman, part of the security, marched up and down. I sat upright on the bench, not knowing what to do, until I saw people in the distance making themselves comfortable to sleep on the benches. I lay down on the bench, using the money bag as a pillow under my head. The bench was hard, and I struggled throughout the night trying to make myself comfortable. Here I was at Hong Kong airport, sleeping on a bench, but I knew GOD had a plan and was aware of everything.

The next day, I woke up as the airport began to get busy. On day two, I gathered my things and went to check for any flights to New Zealand. Throughout the day, I waited at the airport, checking until the afternoon, but there were no flights. I decided to contact the brethren. They told me to take a train and provided the name of the station where I needed to stop. The train would take me downtown to Hong Kong, and once I arrived at the station, I could call them. On the train, I didn't know where I was going and couldn't read the names, as there was no English.

Arriving at the station, I saw a call box and contacted them. They told me to wait, and they were on their way. I thought to myself how GOD takes care of us no matter where we are in the world. His never-failing presence is with us wherever we go, and it's amazing how we cross

SET FREE

paths with people who help us in our time of need. In less than 45 minutes, they arrived. We hopped onto a ferry, crossing the harbor to my accommodation for the night. I thought of my family, my wife, and my children, wondering if they knew where I was. I knew they were praying for me, my protection, and that GOD would make a way. I had good fellowship with the brethren, and they took me out for a meal before leaving me at the hotel.

On day three, the next day, I woke up, and the brethren had directed me on how to board the free bus to the airport. Arriving at the airport, I made my way to the departure board and noticed there was an Air New Zealand flight in the afternoon. I went to Air New Zealand Airways to rebook my flight. The man at the desk looked at me and said my flight had been cancelled.

I looked at him and said, "You cancelled my flight because of insufficient funds. I can show you the money. I have the money." He stood up, looked at me, and told me to wait. He walked towards the back of the office. I couldn't see him, but I could hear him speaking to someone. When he returned, he reissued my boarding pass and ticket to New Zealand. I walked away and found a seat near the boarding gate.

Sitting there, I felt so uneasy, not knowing what was going to happen next after experiencing my boarding pass being torn three days ago. The intercom came on, announcing that all passengers to New Zealand should get ready for boarding and queue up, with business class in one queue and economy in another. The economy line was very long, and I stood towards the back. I could not believe I was finally going to board the plane to New Zealand. It had been a long three days. Our economy queue curved slightly, and I could see a few airport officials standing at the boarding gate entrance. One of the officials, who had torn my boarding pass earlier, was among them. Seeing him again immediately made me feel uncomfortable and uneasy. I wondered what his reaction would be when he saw me, unaware that he had already noticed me.

I watched as he walked to the centre of the economy queue. Suddenly, he came straight towards me. I told myself, "Brian, this is it; it's all over now." He put his hand out, shook my hand, and smiled.

Chapter 12

Holding onto my hand, he said I must come with him. The thoughts racing through my mind were indescribable, as it seemed like a replay of the previous ordeal. He began talking and told me I needed to stand in the business class queue so I could board the plane first. He also mentioned that when I returned to Hong Kong, I should come and see him. I could not understand the friendliness towards me, his approach had changed despite knowing what he had put me through. I stepped on the plane, and when it took off, I knew I was on my way to New Zealand.

Arriving in New Zealand, I went through immigration without any hassles. I knew in my heart that GOD had made a way for me to board the plane. I had reached this far because I trusted GOD, and my wife, children, and family had prayed earnestly for me in South Africa. The believers in Hong Kong were a blessing to me, helping me out, and GOD richly blessed them. It felt like angels were all around me, taking charge of my situation. All the praise and glory go to the Lord, knowing He made it all possible and answered prayers. GOD is good. My wife told me that back home in South Africa, she looked up and saw a plane. Suddenly, a sense of peace and comfort came over her. GOD was assuring her that I had made it and was on my way to New Zealand. She knew I was safe and that GOD had made a way for me.

PART TWO

Part Two
Many Places/Countries

My wife and children left South Africa on the 16th of November, 2003, for New Zealand. I had missed them so much and was overjoyed to see my family again, even happier because this time, we were all going to be together. I loved New Zealand. We settled in, and the weather grew on us, with its rain and cold. I owned a seven-seater Nissan Prairie, which was just right for my big family. GOD provided me with work. I enjoyed New Zealand; we fellowshipped in a church with wonderful people and a pastor who was very dear to us. Occasionally, the pastor would ask me to minister in the church when he would leave for mission work in Papua New Guinea. I was elected as a deacon in this fellowship. I built strong relationships with the people in the assembly, and so did my family. I lived in New Zealand for almost a decade and became a New Zealand citizen, as did the rest of my family.

The economy was not too good, and engineering jobs were more available in Australia. I flew over from New Zealand to Australia for a job, but things did not work out for me. Later, another job opportunity came up, and I tried again and succeeded. I worked away from home for a few months, flying back to New Zealand to see my family. My wife had studied over the years and had become a registered teacher, and our children had thrived and made the most of the opportunities to upskill themselves.

I missed working away from my family and came to a decision: my family needed to join me in Australia. When the time was right, I flew

Chapter 12

to New Zealand, gave up our rental home, sold our furniture, and relocated to New South Wales, Australia. GOD provided me with good employment and a good car. I was able to take care of my family. We rented a good home in the countryside of Maitland.

In New Zealand, I had met a brother at a convention, Bro Joshua, from Sydney, Australia. We became friends during the convention, and he mentioned that if I ever came to Sydney, I should visit their fellowship. He gave me his contact details and the address of the church. Some Sundays, I would travel almost two hours to go to church. It was so worth it; I thoroughly enjoyed the services and the warmth and welcoming spirit of the believers. My wife and I made some good friends and often visited Bro Joshua and his family. The pastor at the fellowship asked me to share the word of GOD whenever we visited. It was so good to be among the brethren; it felt like my church family, and I was encouraged.

I lived in New South Wales for a few months before making my way to Brisbane for better job opportunities. I was offered a job in Brisbane. By faith, my wife desired to live in North Lakes. We relocated and stored all our furniture in a storage unit in North Lakes. I stayed near my job in Brisbane, while my wife went to live with our children on the Sunshine Coast with her sister. While I worked at the new job, my wife applied for rentals in North Lakes. A rental became available in North Lakes. I worked the new job for two weeks when they told me I had to finish because the guy working there was returning from leave. I broke the news to my wife.

Here I was, without a job, and unable to take the rental. I met my wife and children, and we were on our way to pick up the keys for our rental in North Lakes when my mobile rang. I stopped the car and told my wife to continue driving while I took the call. It was an important call from a company offering me a job on the LNG project. This was a job I had applied for a long time ago, and finally, they were corresponding with me. Before I knew it, my start date was given.

By the time my wife parked the car at the agency for the rental, I had secured a job. GOD made a way right at the last minute. GOD

SET FREE

is a miracle-working GOD. It was a fly-in fly-out job, twenty-eight days on and seven days off with my family, for two years. I met many people from all walks of life on this project. We would have church meetings in the evening after work.

I missed my family, but I had a goal to achieve: I desired to buy a home for my family. I believed GOD had provided this job for me because He had a plan for me to purchase a home for my family. We rented for two years, patiently trusting GOD for my finances, wisdom, direction, and making the right choices and decisions.

As I was nearing my goal, I prayed with my wife and asked GOD to lead the way and show us where to buy a home. GOD had brought us this far, and I knew He would see us through. My wife started researching and looking for suburbs where houses were being built. During one of my rest and recovery periods, she said, "Brian, let's take a drive. I want to show you a suburb where they are building houses."

We chatted with a guy at the sales office, and he took us to see a few plots and houses. There was a plot that was still just a piece of land, and I liked it even though it was not road level. When we were leaving, I put my hand out towards it and said, "Lord, I really like this plot and I claim it in the name of Jesus." On June 20, 2015, we moved into our home; GOD gave me the exact house I had desired.

The LNG project was coming to an end, and the same company was going to build another LNG project in Perth, Western Australia. I prayed about this and applied for the welding position on the new project. A month later, while still at Curtis Island in Gladstone, I was made redundant. I spent a blissful month in my new home, feeling so thankful for what GOD had done for me, giving me the opportunity to purchase a home for my family in Australia. GOD had taken care of me, given me good health to work and provide for my family, and made it all possible.

I received a call from the company's recruitment team, providing me with a fly-out date and start date. I arrived in Perth and attended an induction course for the project. I was then flown to Onslow, Western

Chapter 12

Australia, to the construction site and camp, which would be my new home for the next twenty-eight days.

Only two weeks into the job, an accident occurred. I was working with a pipefitter on a scaffold (a tradesman who installs and assembles pipes). He needed to lower the pipe by 100mm, asking me to guide the pipe for him while he went to the back to lower it. We worked in a tent, called a humpy, which was closed on the sides to prevent wind from entering and sparks from exiting while welding or grinding was happening. As I stood there holding the pipe, it moved, and my arm became wedged between two pipes. I tried to free my arm, realising it was jammed. I called out to him to come and lift the pipe off my arm. I looked up and saw him standing above me. He saw what had happened, ran back, and lifted the pipe, releasing my arm.

Pulling my arm out, I saw blood and realised I was bleeding profusely. I didn't fully grasp the severity of my injury. My hand flopped, and I felt unwell. Using one hand, I climbed down the catwalk to get to the ground level. Once there, a leading hand told me to sit down. Feeling faint and in shock, I saw an esky at the base of a column and asked for water. The leading hand handed me water and radioed the medical centre to send an ambulance.

While waiting for the ambulance, I felt weak and faint again, asking for more water. Drinking more water stabilised me a little. When the ambulance arrived, the paramedics attended to my hand and arm, which continued to bleed. I was rushed to the medical centre on site, where they immediately administered morphine for the pain. After an hour, the ambulance took me to the airport, where a lite flight air ambulance jet flew me to Perth in a non-stop two-hour flight.

Upon arrival at the airport, an ambulance was waiting to escort me to a private hospital in Perth. The doctor on the lite flight informed me that I had severed a tendon and fractured a bone, but there was no broken bone, which consoled me. At the hospital, I was admitted for surgery. My wife was contacted and called the hospital to find out the surgery time, requesting a call when the operation was over. She

SET FREE

wanted a quiet moment to pray and trust the Lord for a successful operation.

My wife later mentioned that it was an uneasy time for her, knowing she couldn't be with me. I spent two days in the hospital, and the operation went smoothly, praise GOD. They put a cast on me with twenty-four stitches using staples and a few stitches on my finger. The company booked me into a hotel, where I stayed for a few days, and they picked me up for my check-ups.

Fortunately, my pastor from South Africa was visiting a family in Perth at the time. My wife informed him of my situation, and he, his wife, and a brother came to visit me. Seeing familiar faces made me feel better. We went to the dining area in the hotel, where I bought them dinner, and we had some good fellowship. The pastor prayed for me, and it was great to see him again after such a long time. It was quite a coincidence to be in Perth, injured, and have him visit the country.

I missed my wife and family and requested to be flown back home for treatment. This injury put me out of work for the next nine months. My right hand was injured, making it impossible to work. In the mornings, my hands and fingers would get stiff, and I couldn't close my fist. Sleeping was difficult, especially on my favourite side, so I had to prop my arm on a pillow. My wife would massage my fingers and help me with finger exercises in the mornings.

Months of therapy were needed, and my wife would drive me to these sessions. I was strictly not allowed to drive. My wife was a great support during my injury, taking excellent care of me and assisting with tasks I couldn't manage.

Showering, dressing, eating, holding a cup of tea, writing, and combing my hair—my wife cared for me and helped with everything. GOD was good to me; I continued to receive my wages from the company every week for the next nine months. I had just bought a home, and GOD provided, ensuring my bills were still being met despite my injury. Losing coordination in my hand, I often dropped the coffee cup I was trying to hold. Feeling embarrassed and clumsy, I would spill coffee instead of drinking it. Unable to use my left hand, I struggled.

CHAPTER 12

There were great concerns from the doctors about whether I would be able to weld again. The guy who caused my accident had his services terminated. At one stage during my treatment, the doctor who operated on me needed to see me for a check-up. The company planned to fly me to Perth, but my wife refused. She felt she needed to go with me because I needed help with my hand and arm. The company flew both of us to Perth, covering tickets, hotel accommodation, and transport. They took care of everything.

Arriving at the medical centre, the doctor checked me and was not happy with the condition of my arm and hand. He felt I needed to stay in Perth for the next ten days. My wife and I had understood we would just fly in, see the doctor, and fly back to Queensland. Instead, we found ourselves staying in a hotel for the next ten days. I received intense physio sessions and treatment. Attending the physio sessions in Perth helped my injury progress. Nearing nine months, it was a relief to have no more cast and staples.

Nine months was a long time. Getting back to work felt strange after such a long period. The company put me on light duty, working behind the scenes to get me back to welding. I knew I was not ready. After nine months without welding and recovering from an injury, my performance was not the same. I often wondered how long it would take for me to get back to where I was. Continuing with light duty, I eventually started welding again.

Previously, working on the LNG project at Curtis Island in Queensland for two years, I had built strong relationships with the supervision team, who were very happy with my work ethic and welding record. Now, working for the same company but with different supervision, only two weeks on a new job before the injury didn't give them time to know me and my efficiency in my trade.

The company became nasty towards me, seeing me as injured and not realising this was an accident on the job. The person I worked with caused the accident; I did not bring this upon myself. In my heart, I knew that as a believer, this kind of trial was to be expected. Some of the supervision staff knew I was a Christian and respected me. GOD

SET FREE

gave me victory, and I sensed there was a plot against me. The superintendent was involved with the supervisor to make me uncomfortable on the job. I approached him and asked him to sack (fire) me. He told me he wanted to, but human resources would not allow him to do so. He acknowledged that he knew I was a good person. When he mentioned this, I realised he had been misinformed about me. Later, GOD revealed who the instigator was, causing all this trouble for me on the job. GOD always protected me, giving me wisdom when faced with adversity. The job was coming to an end, and soon there would be a retrenchment. After some thought, I decided to resign and head back home. I missed my family and wanted to be back with them. It was a seven-hour flight to get back home, two hours from Onslow to Perth, and five hours from Perth to Brisbane.

Giving GOD the glory during this time of my injury, He truly took care of me and protected me. I could have lost my arm, but instead, GOD healed me, restored me, and gave me the confidence to return to my welding trade. He blessed me with other jobs after leaving this project. Supervisors and workers admired my work and commented on the quality of my welds. Thank you, Lord, for being there for me. Even in my trade, I was able to provide for my family. GOD constantly proved Himself to me; I was not alone on this journey. GOD was right there all the time. My hope is in the Lord. No matter what I do or attempt to do, He sees me through always.

Chapter 13
The Grace of GOD

Growing up, I did not realise how GOD watched over me. I lived such a carefree and careless life. Now that I am older—a father, husband, and grandad—I truly appreciate the goodness of GOD. In my past life, without Christ, I faced death and dying in a sinful condition. I could have been separated from GOD. Before coming to Christ, always facing violence, death, and challenges, GOD found favour in me. GOD was gracious to me; He chose me. GOD made a way for me and showed me He is the way. In John 14:6 in the Bible, Jesus saith unto Him, "I am the way, the truth, and the life: no man cometh to the Father, but by me." GOD had a plan for my life. He gave to me a wonderful wife who loves GOD—a GOD-fearing woman serving Him.

When I met my wife, many people tried to separate us, but now I know I had found favour with the Lord. Obtaining favour from GOD, He fought the battles for us so His plan could fall into place. You may ask the question: in the condition I was in as a sinner, how could GOD do something for me? It was GOD's love. The Bible says in Romans 5:8-9, "But GOD commendeth His love toward us, in that, while we were yet sinners, Christ died for us. Much more then, being now justified by His blood, we shall be saved from wrath through Him." This does not mean that because Christ died for me, I should remain in sin.

To you, the reader, the Bible says in Acts 2:38, "Repent and be baptised, every one of you, in the name of Jesus Christ for the remission of sins, and ye shall receive the gift of the Holy Ghost." In Romans 6:1, it says, "What shall we say then? Shall we continue in sin, that grace may

SET FREE

abound?" Ask yourself the question: how much grace do you have? It's not worth continuing in sin. Romans 6:2 says, "GOD forbid. How shall we that are dead to sin live any longer therein?"

I have been serving the Lord for over forty years. Serving GOD has brought great joy into my life. Sometimes I wonder if only I had known GOD when I was younger, perhaps I would not have lived such a careless and carefree life. But then I question whether I would appreciate GOD the way I do now. It was GOD's grace and love towards me, knowing I did not deserve it. GOD looked beyond my faults and saw my needs. Letting go of resentment and anger towards those who hurt me was something I had to learn. On this journey, I learned how to forgive. The Bible says in Ephesians 4:32, "And be ye kind one to another, tender-hearted, forgiving one another, even as GOD for Christ's sake hath forgiven you." Through forgiveness, I developed feelings of understanding, empathy, and compassion towards those who hurt me. I felt freedom, delivered from resentment, setting me free in my spirit.

In the world, if anyone harmed me, revenge would be my first thought. Now, I get on my knees and fervently pray for them instead. Serving the Lord gave me a blessed assurance; I am always at peace with GOD. His grace changed my life. I cannot explain what a blessing it is to serve GOD. Over the years, my wife and I have allowed our children to experience the goodness of GOD. To the reader, friends, don't put off making your peace with GOD. The time is now, before it is too late. When it is time to cross over, we need to be sure we know where we are going. Remember, on that day, no one is going to stand with you if you don't accept Jesus Christ as your personal saviour and repent from your sins. The Bible says in 1 Timothy 2:5, "For there is one GOD, and one mediator between GOD and men, the man Christ Jesus."

There is a way, it is GOD's provided way. Proverbs 14:12 says, "There is a way which seemeth right unto a man, but the end thereof are the ways of death." In 1 Kings 22, we read the story of King Ahab, who wanted to take over the city of Ramoth Gilead.

The Syrians were in control at the time, and it seemed right in King Ahab's eyes to take the city. GOD had a prophet go to him and tell

Chapter 13

him what would happen if he went ahead. King Ahab believed his decision to take Ramoth Gilead was right, so he went into war with the Syrians and died. GOD always warns people before judgment. Ahab did not heed GOD's word from the prophet. When we look around in the world today, we see leaders of nations doing the same thing. In the Bible, Exodus 20:13 says, "Thou shalt not kill." This is what the word of GOD says. These leaders send their armies into neighbouring countries, killing people. To these leaders, they are doing the right thing, but many innocent people are dying. Look at Russia and Ukraine, and other countries fighting against each other—the end result is only death.

Coming closer to home, our families and friends don't like the idea of being corrected. When feuds or issues arise among family or friends, each one tries to prove they are right. The Bible says in Romans 3:4, "GOD forbid: yea, let GOD be true, but every man a liar; as it is written." We need to judge a matter by the word of GOD. The scripture continues to say, "That thou mightest be justified in thy sayings, and mightest overcome when thou art judged." King Ahab did not listen and did not heed GOD's word.

There was another man in the Bible who believed what was right to him. Read Luke 16:19-31. This was a rich man who materially needed nothing. He lived a sumptuous life. In his eyes, riches were all that mattered, not realising the very breath GOD gave him to live. Looking at his riches, he was still not satisfied and decided to build greater barns and accumulate more riches. The Bible says in Proverbs 14:12, "There is a way which seemeth right unto a man, but the end thereof are the ways of death." That night, GOD said, "Thou fool, this night thy soul is required of thee." He did not know he was going to die.

A beggar named Lazarus would sit by this rich man's gate, full of sores. He was so hungry, desiring to be fed with the crumbs that fell off the rich man's table. Even the dogs would come and lick his sores. The rich man did not care about Lazarus, the beggar; instead, he worried about his riches. Lazarus the beggar died and was carried into Abraham's bosom. The rich man also died and was buried, finding himself in hell, tormented. The rich man looked up and far off, he could see Abraham and Lazarus in his bosom. Here, the rich man was being tormented in hell. He cried out to Abraham, who was on the other side, and said, "Please, Abraham, can you send Lazarus to dip the tip of his finger in water? I am tormented." When he was alive, the rich man did not care about Lazarus sitting at the gate, poor and hungry. Abraham answered the rich man and said, "There is a gulf between us; we cannot come to you, neither can you come to us." Our time to make our peace with GOD is now, so we do not find ourselves in the position of the rich man.

The Bible says in Deuteronomy 15:11: "For the poor shall never cease out of the land: therefore, I command thee, saying, Thou shalt open thine hand wide unto thy brother, to thy poor, and to thy needy, in thy land." The rich man enjoying his life seemed right in his own eyes. It brought him joy to have all the riches and live a sumptuous life. However, there is only joy in the Lord, which gives us strength. There is a way that leads to destruction, and there is a way that leads to life.

The Bible says in Matthew 7:13-14: "Enter ye in at the strait gate: for wide is the gate, and broad is the way that leadeth to destruction, and many there be which go in thereat. Because strait is the gate, and narrow is the way, which leadeth unto life, and few there be that find it." There is only one way. John 14:6 says, "Jesus saith unto him, I am the way, the truth, and the life: no man cometh unto the Father, but by me." We must be born again, becoming a new creature in Christ Jesus. Jesus says in John 3:3: "Verily, verily, I say unto thee, Except a man be born again, he cannot see the kingdom of heaven."

We must be born of water and the Spirit. John 3:5 says, "Jesus answered, Verily, verily, I say unto thee, Except a man be born of water and of the Spirit, he cannot enter into the kingdom of GOD." You must repent and be baptised, as the Bible says in Acts 2:38: "Repent, and be baptised every one of you in the name of Jesus Christ for the remission of sins, and ye shall receive the gift of the Holy Ghost." The only way is GOD's way. John 14:1-6 starts with: "Let not your heart be troubled: ye believe in GOD, believe also in me." In verse 6, Jesus says, "I am the way, the truth, and the life."

Chapter 13

To the reader, serving the Lord Jesus Christ has been the best part of my life. I will serve the Lord until He takes me home. It is a great joy to serve GOD. GOD is the centre of our joy. I trust and pray that you make the decision to be born again. This is the way. Allow GOD to come into your life, and you too can be set free.

Chapter 14
The Overcomer

Going all the way with Christ is the only way we will overcome by faith. The Bible says in 1 John Chapter 5:3-5: "For this is the love of GOD, that we keep his commandments. For whatsoever is born of GOD overcometh the world: and this is the victory that overcometh the world, even our faith. Who is he that overcometh the world, but he that believeth that Jesus is the Son of GOD?" I see GOD soaking these verses in love, like honey, making it sweet to people. We must allow the Spirit of GOD to come and saturate us with His love.

When GOD is speaking to us, His motive is that we project His love. GOD conquered the enemy with love. Don't ever undermine yourself. Do not belittle the value GOD has placed in you. GOD valued you and me so much that He laid down His life for us. The enemy comes in different forms: someone close to you, a family member, workplace; he will come and praise you, get you to a point that is not pleasing in the eyes of GOD. The enemy can come in the form of money, people, and popularity. It is not about being elevated because there is nothing you can do without GOD. This fight is a fight to the end. We fight principalities of darkness. Principalities of darkness cannot bear the light. GOD can allow you to overcome. GOD can see the unseen.

The sun sends piercing rays through the darkness to bring forth the light. We are that light, and this light allows us to move forward. When we are born of GOD, we overcome the world by faith. The victory here

Chapter 14

is that you are born of GOD. My prayer for you and me is that GOD gives us grace and wisdom, and that the mind of Christ be in us to face and overcome the situations in our lives. The Bible says in 1 John 4:4: "Ye are of GOD, little children, and have overcome them: because greater is he that is in you, than he that is in the world." We are people of faith, not of sight. GOD wants us to humble ourselves and come before Him. The Bible says in 1 Peter 5:6: "Humble yourselves therefore under the mighty hand of GOD, that he may exalt you in due time." We must show GOD that we love Him and be obedient. If you are obedient, GOD will take care of the rest. Sometimes we condemn ourselves, thinking very little of ourselves, feeling unworthy. GOD wants us to trust Him. Our victory does not lie in vengeance; we do not seek vengeance. The Bible says in Romans 12:19: "Dearly beloved, avenge not yourselves, but rather give place unto wrath: for it is written, Vengeance is mine; I will repay, saith the Lord."

Make GOD your habitation and live in His presence. May GOD give you the desire to fear Him and to do what He wants in your life. The fear of the Lord is the beginning of wisdom. Psalm 34:11 says: "Come, ye children, hearken unto me: I will teach you the fear of the Lord." There is no price you can put on GOD's care for you and me. Psalm 34:7 says: "The angel of the Lord encampeth round about them that fear him, and delivereth them." GOD promises He will take care of us. 1 Peter 5:7 says: "Casting all your care upon him, for he careth for you." You are the apple of GOD's eye and cannot be touched. Zechariah 2:8 says: "For thus saith the Lord of hosts; After the glory hath he sent me unto the nations which spoiled you: for he that toucheth you toucheth the apple of his eye." The way we live our lives and conduct ourselves shows GOD that we care for Him. Psalm 34:13-14 says: "Keep thy tongue from evil, and thy lips from speaking guile. Depart from evil, and do good; seek peace, and pursue it."

Reading an article about two men in 1829, George Wilson and James Porter committed crimes and were both sentenced in 1830 to execution by hanging. Porter was executed, but Wilson's execution was set for a later date. Influential friends pleaded for mercy to the President

SET FREE

of the United States. Andrew Jackson, on behalf of the president, issued a formal pardon, dropping all charges except for twenty years for other crimes Wilson committed. George Wilson refused the pardon. The United States Supreme Court determined that the court could not give the prisoner the benefit of the pardon unless he claimed the benefit of it. He may accept it or not as he pleases. A pardon is an act of grace. The Lord Jesus made a way on the cross of Calvary for us all that we may be pardoned. If we reject our pardon, the Bible says the wages of sin is death, but the gift of GOD is eternal life. 1 John 1:9 says: "If we confess our sins, he is faithful and just to forgive us our sins and to cleanse us from all unrighteousness." John 8:36 says: "If the Son therefore shall make you free, you shall be free indeed." Only the Lord Jesus Christ can *SET FREE*.

THE END

Reference

All scripture and quotes are from the King James Version in the HOLY BIBLE.

LII/Legal information Institute https://www.lawcornell.edu> text George Wilson

Epilogue

Brian lives in Australia, continuing to love the Lord Jesus Christ with all his heart. GOD has blessed him with good health, and he travels every day to work as a special class welder. Brian is very precise, conscientious, and passionate about his trade. Recently, he jokingly remarked, "The older I become, the better my welding becomes."

His children live close by with their families, and it brings Brian great joy to see his children love the Lord. He is particularly moved when his grandchildren request to pray, sing a song, attempt to play an instrument, and mention the name Jesus.

Brian continues to be a witness in his workplace among his peers, sharing the gospel. He lives a balanced life through fasting and praying, which is how GOD intervenes in his life, meeting his spiritual needs and strengthening his faith, helping him overcome when storms arise. Together with his wife, GOD has provided them with their own house, a place they can call home. Here, their children and grandchildren have a sense of belonging and know they are always welcome. It is a place they too can call home, a retreat during tough times where they can be spiritually encouraged and feel the presence and joy of the Lord.

Sharon Crick

1981 Amardah Shipyards, Bayhead. I worked on this Oil rig Durban, South Africa built for America. My second Oil rig job.

Me, in the street of Hong Kong during my 3 day stay. One of the brethren who came to my aid.

SET FREE

1980 November the happiest day of my life, marrying the love of my life. Forty four years later, we are still happy ever after. A Christ centered marriage has been our foundation, pleasing to GOD and to each other.

Northgate Primary school, class of 47. In the circle is me.

Chapter 14

1999 My beautiful family. Far right my daughter Lydia, eldest daughter Liesel, myself, my youngest daughter Sarah, my son Seth and my wife Sharon. This photo was a request from one of the brethren, he asked if he could please take a family photo after the open-air church meeting. I would attend these meetings, along with my family, on a Saturday morning witnessing to people on the streets of Durban, South Africa. Saturday mornings were a dedicated morning unto the Lord, winning souls for Christ.

2005 New Zealand, me setting the welding machaine before welding.

2011 me and my wife in New Zealand. The following year 2012 we relocated to Australia.

Me, at fourteen years old, growing not knowing what was laying ahead of me. GOD had a plan, for my life at the time, I did not know about.

Chapter 14

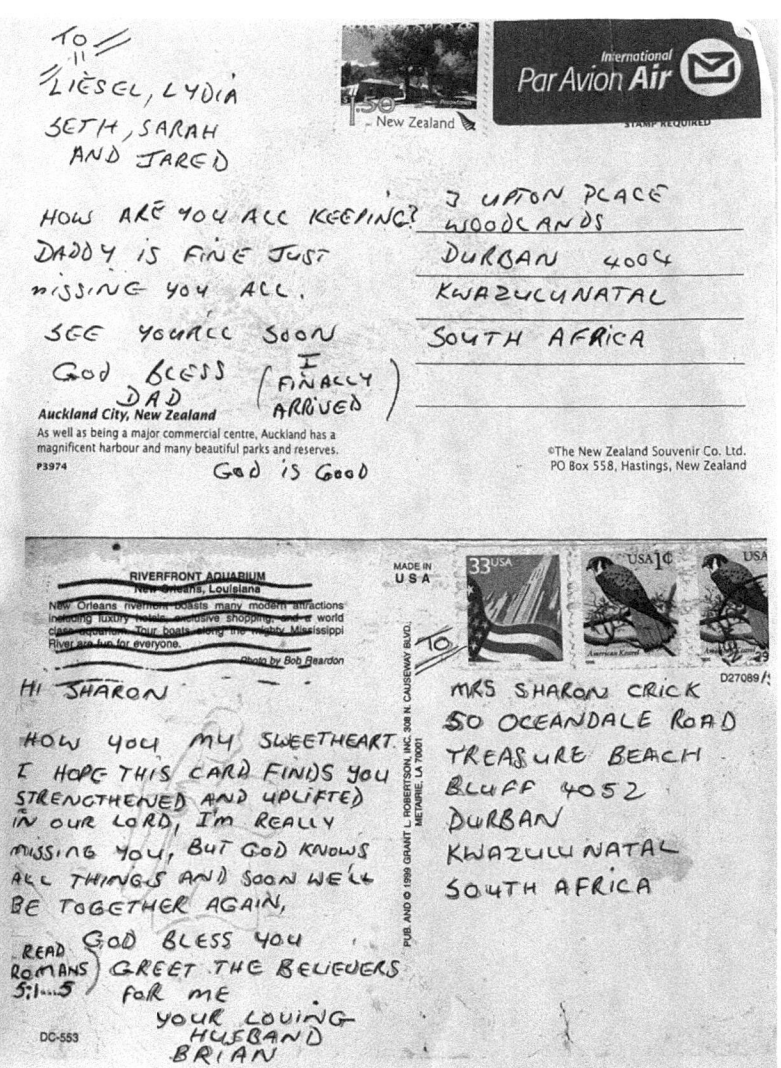

I had no choice when it came to my trade. Took me to different places/ countries and I missed my family. A letter to my children assuring them I was safe, and I missed them from New Zealand. A letter to my darling wife Sharon, it was hard on her, me not being around and I knew my post cards will bring some comfort to her, from New Orleans, America.

www.ingramcontent.com/pod-product-compliance
Lightning Source LLC
Chambersburg PA
CBHW050248120526
44590CB00016B/2263